WINNERS

CIRCLE

MUSIC

THE BUSINESS BLUEPRINT
FOR MUSIC PRODUCERS

KASH JOHNS

INDEX

ABOUT THE AUTHOR

Kash Johns is a renowned music producer, manager, music publisher, and visionary whose impact on the major music industry spans over a decade. Known for his extraordinary knack for identifying and cultivating new talent, Kash has a record that speaks to his unwavering dedication to excellence, creativity, and strategic insight. As the CEO of **Winners Circle Music & Publishing**, and through his partnership with Warner Chappell Publishing, Kash has consistently pioneered new paths in the music industry, helping producers and artists navigate the often complex and competitive landscape of the major music business.

Kash's journey began with a passion for creating beats. He initially built his reputation by brokering beats online, earning music placements, and eventually establishing himself as a trusted industry mentor at music conferences. His first breakthrough came with **Go Grizzly**, a 17-year-old producer from Atlanta. Kash's guidance and connections led Go Grizzly to secure a publishing deal with a major publisher, propelling him into the spotlight. This early success demonstrated Kash's ability to nurture young talent and prepare them for the challenges of the industry.

Kash's career trajectory continued to rise as he discovered and signed **Smash David**. Under Kash's management, Smash David rose to work with some of the biggest pop stars in the world, eventually securing a publishing partnership with one of the industry's major players and achieving receiving 14 Grammy nominations.

Other notable signings include **Pooh Beatz**, a Detroit-based producer who skyrocketed to over 200 major music placements and three Grammy nominations; and the Grammy-winning songwriter/ producer **London Jae** from Atlanta. Kash's clients have consistently remarkable success, setting new standards in the industry, with eighty-three #1 hits on the Billboard Top 40 and over 30 Grammy nominations.

Driven by a deep-rooted passion for music and a commitment to empowering the next generation, Kash uses his experience to uplift aspiring producers. He believes that the right combination of strategy, resilience, and creative insight can turn ambition into success. Through this playbook, Kash aims to provide readers with essential tools, actionable insights, and the winning mindset needed to excel in today's major music industry and realize their dreams.

INTRODUCTION: UNDERSTANDING THE LANDSCAPE

The major music industry, much like the world of professional sports, is an intensely competitive arena where only the most prepared, skilled, and strategically minded individuals rise to the top. While athletes benefit from clear-cut guidelines, rigorous training, and structured systems that help them master the "rules of the game," aspiring music producers often find themselves navigating a complex and uncharted landscape without those guidelines made readily available. This book is designed to change that.

Winners Circle Music: The Business Blueprint for Music Producers serves as your practical guide, illuminating the often-opaque world of music production and providing you with the tools and knowledge necessary to thrive. Just as there are various levels in sports—where each tier offers unique challenges and rewards--the music industry presents its own levels of success, with the major labels equivalent to the major leagues as the pinnacle of achievement.

Much like an enthusiastic basketball fan who dreams of making it to the NBA, many music enthusiasts aspire to create and share their art, even if they may never step onto a major stage.

This playbook is for those who are ready to transition from mere admirers of music to empowered creators who understand the ins and outs of the industry.

Throughout this journey, we will explore crucial topics such as securing publishing agreements, negotiating royalties, and leveraging collaboration. Each chapter will provide practical insights, firsthand experiences, and actionable strategies that will empower you to carve your path in the major music industry.

As we set out on this adventure together, remember just as athletes train for peak performance, you too can cultivate your skills and knowledge to shape a legacy in major music business. Let us dive in and get started on your journey to becoming a successful major music producer!

PURPOSE OF THE BOOK

For aspiring and seasoned music producers alike, the lack of transparency in the industry can lead to costly mistakes and missed opportunities. Without a clear set of guidelines, many talented producers stumble not because of a lack of ability but because they simply are not equipped with the right knowledge or strategy to navigate industry demands.

This book is here to serve as a comprehensive guide—a rulebook that translates the complexities of the music business into actionable steps.

Just as a sports coach teaches plays, strategies, and mental discipline, this guide will help producers gain clarity on the business side of their craft, setting them up to make informed decisions and establish successful careers.

I remember when I first started out, feeling overwhelmed by the intricacies of contracts and negotiations. After making one mistake, I realized the importance of having a solid understanding of the business side of music. It was a pivotal moment that shaped my approach and led to significant successes for both myself, the music producers, and the songwriters I worked with.

By following the strategies outlined in this book, you will be better equipped to avoid common pitfalls. For instance, one of my clients was able to secure a lucrative publishing deal after applying negotiation techniques I shared with him. This not only boosted his income but also helped him build valuable relationships within the industry.

As you embark on this journey, remember that success is not just about talent; it is about knowledge and strategy. I encourage you to engage actively with the content, take notes, and apply what you learn. The insights within these pages have the potential to transform your career and enable you to leave a lasting mark on the music industry.

SPORTS ANALOGY: WHY PROFESSIONALISM MATTERS

Think again about professional sports. Every player, coach, and manager in sports understands their role, follows established practices, and adheres to a structure. Athletes know what is required to succeed at each stage, whether it is training regimens, contractual agreements, or the fundamentals of teamwork. They have coaches to mentor them, leagues with rules, and structured paths from amateur to professional status. This framework makes it possible for athletes to thrive, understand their place in the game, and advance their careers with purpose.

In contrast, the major music industry lacks this kind of structure, particularly for producers. While managers and label executives each play crucial roles, the pathways to success are not always clear, and opportunities for mentorship are limited. Producers are often left to learn through trial and error, navigating by instinct rather than guidance. This lack of structure and support can lead to misunderstandings, undervalued work, and challenging career hurdles.

By establishing a framework for success, this book seeks to bridge that gap. It will lay out the rules of the game, define roles and responsibilities, highlight common missteps, and offer strategies for success.

The goal is to create a blueprint for music production that enables producers to approach their careers with the same discipline, foresight, and professionalism that athletes use to reach their peak potential.

KEY THEMES TO EXPECT

Defining the Game:

Just as athletes need to know the rules of their sport, producers must understand industry's basic contracts, rights, and revenue. This book will lay out these essential "rules of engagement."

Building a Winning Team:

In sports, a dedicated team is essential for success. Similarly, producers must collaborate effectively with artists, managers, and other key players. This book will emphasize the importance of networking and building a support team.

Crafting a Strategy:

Like sports teams that devise game plans to win, music producers need to create strategies for branding, revenue, and career progression. This book will offer insights into building a personal brand, understanding market trends, and navigating industry challenges.

Learning from Mistakes:

Sports teams review game footage to learn from losses. Producers can benefit from case studies that show both triumphs and setbacks in the music business, enabling them to avoid common pitfalls.

By the end of this book, readers will possess the tools, knowledge, and confidence necessary to make calculated decisions, avoid common pitfalls, and unlock the success they are truly capable of achieving. Just as professional sports rely on discipline, strategy, and teamwork, so too does the major music industry.

Welcome to the ultimate playbook for music producers. Are you ready to leverage the RR formula? By combining Real Relationships with Real Results, you will be well on your way to achieving the kind of success that can lead you to your very own Rolls-Royce lifestyle. I promise you, with dedication and the right approach, the possibilities are limitless!

CHAPTER 1:
THE RULES OF THE GAME:
CONTRACTS AND RIGHTS

Entering the major music industry without a solid grasp of contracts and rights is like stepping onto a football field without knowing the rules—one misstep, and you could lose control of the game. For producers, understanding these foundational concepts is essential to protecting their work, getting compensated, and building a sustainable career. In this chapter, we will demystify the basic "rules of the game" by breaking down the most essential elements of contracts, royalties, distribution, and publishing rights.

Just as a coach lays out plays and explains the objective of each position, we will present these ideas in a clear, step-by-step manner so you can make informed decisions every time you enter into an agreement or release track.

UNDERSTANDING CONTRACTS: THE FRAMEWORK OF YOUR CAREER

Contracts are the foundation of every professional relationship in the music industry. They define the obligations, rights, and expectations of each party, much like playbooks set the terms and roles for a game. But not all contracts are the same; different agreements serve different purposes. Here is an overview of the key contract types every producer should know:

1. PRODUCER AGREEMENTS:

A producer's agreement defines the terms under which a producer creates and delivers music for an artist or label. Key elements include payment terms, royalty splits, and intellectual property rights. These agreements typically specify whether the producer will receive an upfront fee, a percentage of future royalties, or a combination of both.

In the past, the music industry often told producers that it was the job of their manager or lawyer to oversee the details of these agreements. But I am here to tell you something different: **It is your job to understand these terms and know how to negotiate them.** Just as an NFL player would not leave their contract negotiations entirely to their agent, you should not leave your financial future up to someone else.

To succeed, you must understand your value, because **the more you learn, the more you earn.** Do not settle for an agreement that undervalues your contributions. If you are a top-tier producer with a unique sound, negotiate as such. **Know your worth and demand it.**

At the same time, do not ask for a fee or royalty percentage that you obviously do not deserve. Just like in the NFL, if a player overestimates their worth, they risk getting laughed out of the negotiation room. You must be realistic and recognize the level of your talent.

The key is balance. Asking for an amount that reflects your talent, and experience will ensure you are taken seriously. And if you are new to the game, focus on building a reputation and proving your worth before asking for top-tier rates.

A producer who learns the business side—**the contract negotiation side**—is a producer who is setting themselves up for long-term success.

2. RECORDING AGREEMENTS:

Recording agreements primarily exist between artists and record labels, but they also impact producers—especially regarding ownership of the master recordings. On the major label side, the record label typically owns the masters, while producers negotiate a percentage of publishing and backend royalties. In independent deals, producers often have more leverage to negotiate ownership or a percentage of the masters, depending on their contribution and bargaining power. Understanding these distinctions is critical for producers to ensure they maximize their long-term earnings.

For producers, **this is where the concept of a "production deal" comes into play**. A production deal allows a producer to sign an artist to a contract where the producer has the right to negotiate on behalf of the artist for their major recording deal with a label.

Think of it like an NBA agent representing a player during the draft. The agent does not just sit back and hope for a good deal; they work tirelessly to negotiate the best contract for their client. They play a pivotal role in ensuring that the player's value is recognized, their rights are protected, and they secure a deal that sets them up for success. Similarly, a producer with a production deal has leverage and the ability to negotiate a major label recording agreement on behalf of the artist they have signed—securing a better deal not only for the artist but also for themselves.

The producer, much like an agent, can help guide the artist through the negotiation process, ensure fair terms are in place, and maximize potential royalties. If the artist succeeds, so does the producer. It is a symbiotic relationship, where both parties stand to benefit from a successful deal.

In essence, **a production deal is your chance to act as the "agent" for your artist**—negotiating the recording contract, ensuring that you retain a fair share of the masters, and setting yourself up for future royalties. This is not just about making beats—it is about positioning yourself as a key player in the artist's career and ensuring that you engage in the big money deals that follow.

3. PUBLISHING AGREEMENTS: YOUR GUIDE TO INCOME AND OWNERSHIP

In the music industry, a publishing contract is like a professional athlete's contract—it defines ownership, rights, and earnings from compositions, including melody, lyrics, and structure. Just as a sports agent ensures an athlete gets paid for their performance and endorsements, music publishers manage the collection and distribution of royalties for songwriters and producers. When producers contribute to songwriting, they secure a portion of these royalties, like how an athlete earns revenue from both salary, endorsements, and multiple income streams tied to their contributions.

Publishing deals come in two main formats:

a) Administration Deals

An administration deal, or "admin" deal, allows a major publisher to oversee the collection of royalties, typically for a smaller fee ranging from 10% to 20%. Your lawyer and team will negotiate this rate. Administration deals may or may not include an advance, so it is crucial to evaluate whether the advance fits your current needs and whether the publisher's network and reach aligns with your goals.

b) Co-Publishing Deals

A co-publishing deal means sharing a larger portion of your publishing royalties— usually around 25%, which is half of the so-called publisher's share of the composition— with the major publisher in exchange for an advance. This advance is recoupable, meaning it must be paid back through future royalties before you can earn additional income from your publishing share.

These advances, given to top producers in partnerships with the "Big Three" publishers (Sony, Warner, and Universal), are based on the anticipated success and recoupment potential of the producer's contributions. The largest advances often go to tracks expected to chart well or records where producers have a significant publishing share. However, the recoupment requirement means that producers will only see income from their royalties after the advance is fully paid back.

Contract Structures: MDRC and Multi-Term Contracts

Publishing contracts vary significantly, but they typically fall under two structures:

a) Minimum Delivery and Release Commitment (MDRC)

Under an MDRC, a producer must deliver a certain number of songs that meet agreed-upon release standards to fulfill their contract. This requirement adds pressure to not only create but also ensure these tracks make it to release—a challenge when balancing quality, market appeal, and timelines.

b) Term Contracts

Term contracts outline the number of songs a producer must deliver over a set period. This structure is like an athlete's seasonal commitments; the producer has a set output to meet, often with milestones to trigger further payments. Extended recoupment periods in these agreements allow publishers to collect royalties indefinitely while producers work to satisfy their contractual commitments and qualify for future advances.

The challenge for producers lies in maintaining consistent output while aiming for commercial success, as delays in recoupment affect future payouts and opportunities to negotiate better deals. This dynamic requires a sharp focus on balancing creativity with productivity to build a sustainable career.

Legacy and Long-Term Influence

Just like athletes who leave lasting legacies by retiring their jerseys or maintaining team affiliations, producers have opportunities to shape their legacy. Retaining control over their catalog and intellectual property allows producers to extend their influence, ensuring their music's longevity and ongoing revenue.

The shift to digital and streaming has transformed the music landscape, making it easier for producers to reach a global audience and recoup advances through digital royalties.

Today, producers can build their own brand—just like athletes—by actively engaging with fans, highlighting their work, and monetizing content. By strategically releasing producer-tagged beats, collaborating with rising artists, and maintaining a presence on platforms like YouTube, TikTok, and Instagram, producers can turn viral moments into business opportunities. Streaming playlists, beat stores, and direct-to-consumer marketing further allow producers to bypass traditional industry gatekeepers and create independent revenue streams.

Top producers who partner with major publishers often go a step further, bringing up-and-coming talent under their own imprints. This mentorship role enables them to build a legacy, benefiting from the success of emerging artists while shaping the future of the industry. Through strategic partnerships and publishing agreements, successful producers can eventually transition from creators to executives, much like athletes who retire and move into management or ownership roles.

Personal Experience

When I first negotiated a publishing agreement, my client and I were thrilled to sign our first co-publishing deal with a major publisher. The advance seemed like a huge step forward—validation that we had entered the "big leagues" of music publishing. However, we quickly learned the reality of recoupment. The contract required my client to pay back the advance entirely from his publishing royalties before seeing any real income. Each quarter, his statements showed earnings, but most of that money went straight toward paying off the advance. For two years, he was creating hits but still felt financially stuck.

This became a pivotal lesson: taking a large advance can feel like a win, but without proper planning, it can also put you in a position where your own catalog is working against you. Because of this experience, we approached future deals differently.

Instead of just focusing on the advance amount, we looked deeper into the percentage of ownership my client would retain, how quickly he could recoup, and whether the deal allowed him to retain leverage for future negotiations.

Fast forward to today—after executing three major publishing deals, my client is now a multi-millionaire and signing his own roster of producers. The transparency we had from that first deal—understanding exactly how the recoupment process worked and strategizing around ownership— allowed him to build a catalog that generates long-term wealth instead of just chasing short-term payouts.

Now, when I advise newer producers, I stress this lesson: a big advance doesn't always mean a good deal. Knowing your options and structuring agreements with long-term control in mind can mean the difference between a few years of work and a lifetime of influence.

4. LICENSING AGREEMENTS:

In the music industry, licensing agreements are akin to endorsement deals in professional sports, allowing a song to be used in various media—such as films, commercials, and video games. Specifically, these are called "synchronization" or "synch" licenses, which is discussed further below. These agreements provide a substantial revenue stream for producers, much like endorsements and sponsorships do for athletes.

Licensing is managed by the artist's publisher or record label, who navigate these opportunities and negotiate the terms. Major music producers should always negotiate to retain ownership interest in the compositions to really benefit from both streams of income from a synch license: master and composition/pub royalties.

For clarity and fair compensation, negotiating licensing splits and terms upfront is crucial. This ensures all parties understand their share when a song is commercially licensed, preventing disputes down the line. Just as athletes work with top agencies to secure the best endorsement deals and maximize their earnings, producers often partner with one of the 'Big Three' publishers.

These publishers provide the global infrastructure needed to collect royalties worldwide and secure high-profile placements, increasing both earnings and visibility.

The international reach of the Big Three means they can offer both exclusive and non-exclusive licenses across various territories, maximizing exposure and income from different regions. Additionally, different media (like commercials versus video games) often involve distinct licensing rates, and these publishers are experts at negotiating the best rates based on usage type. This expertise ensures that producers get the highest possible value for their work across multiple platforms.

Finally, licensing deals also impact a producer's brand image, much like endorsement deals affect an athlete's public profile. The Big Three's extensive network provides access to high-visibility, selective placements that align with a producer's image and artistic vision. By collaborating with a top publisher, producers can focus on their craft while leveraging a global powerhouse to secure and manage profitable licensing agreements worldwide.

5. PRODUCER ROYALTIES: YOUR "SCORECARD" IN THE GAME

Royalties are how you get paid for the music you create. There are multiple types of royalties in the industry, each representing a different use of your work. Here is a breakdown:

a) Mechanical Royalties:

Mechanical royalties in the music industry are like ticket and broadcast revenues in Major League Baseball, generated whenever music is reproduced—whether physically on CDs or vinyl, or digitally through downloads and streams. Publishers collect and distribute these royalties to songwriters and producers, providing a valuable income stream for those involved in the songwriting process. However, physical music sales are now primarily sustained by the top 1% of artists, those with massive, loyal fan bases.

Superstars like Taylor Swift, Beyoncé, and Drake are among the few who consistently drive high physical sales, thanks to fans who seek out special or collectible editions of their work. This die-hard fan support mirrors the loyalty of MLB fans who buy season tickets and exclusive memorabilia year after year.

For most artists, digital streaming—like TV/streaming broadcast revenue in baseball—has become the main source of mechanical royalties. Just as the MLB increasingly relies on televised and online viewership to reach a broad audience, the music industry depends on streaming platforms to generate steady royalties.

This shift illustrates how both fields have adapted to digital platforms as their primary revenue sources, while only the industry's superstars continue to succeed in the physical market with collector's editions and exclusive releases.

b) Performance Royalties:

Performance royalties in the music industry are akin to the revenue generated from live games and broadcasts in Major League Baseball. These royalties are earned whenever a song is played publicly, whether on the radio, during concerts, or on streaming services.

Performing Rights Organizations (PROs) like ASCAP, BMI, and SESAC function as the league's governing bodies, collecting these performance royalties, and ensuring fair distribution to songwriters, producers, and other rights holders whenever their music is publicly performed. PROs monitor performances across various platforms to ensure that all parties receive their due compensation.

A key feature of performance royalties is their global nature; artists can earn royalties from performances that occur worldwide. This global reach adds another layer of potential income for successful musicians, especially those with international recognition.

The rise of digital streaming has also transformed the landscape of performance royalties, as more listeners consume music online rather than through traditional radio.

Additionally, live performances remain a vital source of performance royalties, just as attendance at games contributes significantly to a team's overall revenue. Artists who tour frequently and draw large crowds benefit from these live performance royalties, highlighting the connection between audience engagement and earnings in both the music and sports industries.

In summary, the strength of an artist's brand and their audience's loyalty play crucial roles in maximizing performance royalties, much like the factors that influence a team's ticket sales and broadcast revenues in the competitive landscape of MLB.

c) Sync Royalties:

Synchronization or sync royalties are earned when a song is synchronized with visual media, such as movies, television shows, or advertisements. These deals can be highly lucrative for artists and producers, as they typically involve two key components: an upfront licensing fee paid for the right to use the song and backend royalties that are earned each time the media featuring song aired or streamed.

The appeal of sync license royalties lies in there for significant income. The upfront fee compensates the rights holders immediately for granting permission to use the song, while the backend royalties can provide ongoing revenue as the media continues to be broadcast or viewed over time.

This dual income stream makes sync deals an attractive opportunity for songwriters and producers, as successful placements in popular media can lead to enhanced visibility and additional revenue from increased music sales or streaming as audiences discover the song.

Having a major music publisher is crucial for accessing these lucrative sync opportunities. Major publishers have established relationships with film studios, advertising agencies, and video game developers, positioning them to secure high-profile placements in sought-after projects like movie scores, Super Bowl commercials, or NBA Finals advertisements.

These strategic partnerships not only enhance the likelihood of securing prominent sync deals but also ensure that artists receive the best possible terms for their work.

Furthermore, the use of music in visual media can create powerful associations between the song and the content, often leading to increased fan engagement and broader market reach. As such, sync royalties represent not only a financial opportunity but also a strategic avenue for artists to expand their presence in the entertainment industry.

d) Maximizing Your Earnings

Producers can earn royalties directly from an artist or label, supplementing any upfront fees and creating a substantial income stream depending upon the commercial success of a recording. As the creative force behind the production of a song or album, producers oversee elements such as arrangement, sound design, and engineering, all of which contribute to the song's commercial appeal. These contributions justify the producer's share of the masters revenue, which is typically negotiated within the producer agreement and usually start at a minimum of 3% of the published price to dealers ("PPD") or wholesale list price. This number might be around 15% -25% of the artist's net revenue on the exploitation of the masters, if the artist is independent or being accounted to a "net income" "basis from sales, streams, or performances revenues.

Consider this process as an NBA player negotiating their contract. Just as a star player expects a fair percentage of the team's revenue based on their skill and performance, producers should negotiate a fair share that reflects the value they add to the project. While the industry standard is often cited to be around 3% PPD, top-tier producers have the leverage to negotiate for as much as 7% PPD, based on their record and the project's potential. For instance, if a producer's work is expected to be a hit single, a higher percentage is warranted compared to a song with less certain commercial appeal.

Market trends play a significant role here as well. Producer royalties can vary depending on whether the project is released by an indie label or a major label; larger labels typically have the budgets to support higher "all in" royalty rates to the artist and larger marketing and promotion funds, as well as broader distribution. In the current industry landscape, successful producers like Dr. Dre or Max Martin can command premium percentages thanks to their high-profile portfolios and consistent records of success. Producers should also consider the potential for backend earnings from royalties on future sales, licensing deals, or sync placements, which can add significantly to their overall income from a hit project. Negotiating a lucrative producer agreement is thus essential for establishing a sustainable career, as it not only secures upfront income but also builds long-term financial stability.

Personal Experience

Early in my career, I learned how crucial it is to negotiate fair producer royalties. One of my first big negotiations was for a promising young major music producer who had just started working with an A-list artist. The initial offer was for 3 points, but knowing the track had real chart potential, we countered 5 points.

Here is the tricky part: The artist's attorney will typically push back hard on this since any points a producer receives come directly from the artist's share. If an artist only has fifteen points on a song, and we are asking for five, that leaves the artist with just ten points. In practical terms, fifteen points are 15% of 100%, meaning that for every $1 million the song earns, the artist is entitled to $150,000. So, if a producer receives five points from the artist's fifteen, that will break down to $50,000 for the producer, and $100,000 for the artist. Understanding this breakdown makes it clear why it is critical to negotiate smartly and selectively choose artists to build a career with.

After several rounds of back-and-forth, we successfully closed the deal at 5 points. This experience was eye-opening, showing me firsthand how even a single percentage point can mean thousands of dollars if a track hits big. It underscored the importance of identifying a project's potential and firmly advocating for the value you bring to the table.

Today, that major music producer is one of the top names in the industry and now commands even higher points thanks to a proven record. Since then, I have ensured that every major music producer I work with fully understands the worth of their contributions. It is about more than just points; it is about knowing when to stand your ground and when to be flexible. With a strategic approach, we have been able to secure deals that evolve with each success, making this a winning strategy repeatedly.

e) Advances: Starting Strong

In addition to royalties, advances play a key role in a producer's earnings. An upfront payment should ideally start at a minimum of $5,000. This initial payment helps secure your position and provides financial stability to focus on creating quality music.

Just as NBA players leverage their skills to negotiate better contracts, producers should advocate for fair compensation that accurately reflects their contributions. While labels may claim to be financially constrained, most major-label artists have an allocated production budget. The real question is whether the artist has earned enough trust from the label to access it. Be prepared to encounter offers that fall below expectations. To gauge what to ask for, consider the artist's status:

- **A-list Artist** (Superstar): $10,00.00 and up
- **B-list Artist:** $5,000 up to $10,000.00
- **C-list Artist:** $5,000 minimum

When negotiating, highlight your prior work and successes to bolster your position. Remember that advances are recoupable, meaning they will be deducted from future earnings before you see additional payments. Understanding this is essential for managing your finances.

Market trends, like the rise of streaming, may also influence advanced amounts. While securing a fair advance is important, building long-term relationships with artists and labels can lead to more valuable collaborations in the future.

Regardless of the artist's tier, approach negotiations confidently, knowing your worth. By being informed and prepared, you can negotiate an advance that reflects your talent and sets you up for lasting success.

Personal Experience

In my early days managing producers, I remember negotiating an advance for a talented client who was new to the major music scene. He was eager to work with an up-and-coming B-list artist, and the label initially offered a $3,500 advance. Knowing the potential of the project—and the work my client put into it, I agree with a request for $5,000. After some back-and forth, they met us halfway at $4,500. It was not the full amount we aimed for, but it still felt like a win, especially since the artist was only starting to build a name.

This experience taught me the importance of standing firm on the value of my client's contributions while also knowing when to compromise. As that artist's popularity grew, we leveraged our early successes to negotiate better terms on future projects. Today, my client's starting advance for a similar artist would be closer to $15,000.00, thanks to the record he is built.

The key takeaway? Do not settle for less than your worth but also recognize when the long-term relationship might be more valuable than the immediate payout. By setting a standard early on, we have built a foundation that allows us to consistently secure higher advances, and success keeps coming.

6. PUBLISHING RIGHTS: THE OWNERSHIP THAT LASTS

Publishing rights encompass the ownership of a song's composition, including the musical notes, melody, and lyrics, separate from the unique master recording. These rights are invaluable, providing a form of long term "ownership" that enables your music to continue generating income over time. Here is why understanding and securing publishing rights is crucial for producers:

a) Ownership of Compositions:

As a producer, if you contribute to the melody, chords, or lyrics of a song, you may qualify for a share of the ownership interest in the composition. These percentage shares entitle you to a portion of the song's publishing revenue, creating an income stream that extends far beyond the initial release. This means that every time the song is performed, streamed, or licensed, you earn royalties, thereby securing your financial future as a music creator.

b) Long-Term Revenue Potential:

Publishing rights provide ongoing revenue potential through mechanical royalties, performance royalties, and sync fees. This long-term income is vital for producers, especially in an industry where the value of streaming and digital distribution continues to grow. By holding onto publishing rights, you ensure that your contributions are financially recognized and rewarded over time.

c) Registering Your Works:

Registering your works with a Performing Rights Organization (PRO) is essential for effectively collecting royalties associated with your publishing rights. This step ensures you receive the compensation you are owed whenever your music is used publicly. Surprisingly, many music collaborators neglect to register their works. Think of registering with a PRO like obtaining a driver's license: a necessary step to operate successfully in the music industry, because you won't get far without it.

There are three major PROs: ASCAP, BMI, and SESAC. Each performs similar functions but has unique advantages. It is crucial to choose the one that aligns best with your career goals in the major music business. Once you are signed to a major music publisher, they typically oversee the registration of songs with your PRO on your behalf. However, it is still your responsibility to verify that your songs are listed correctly on the PRO's portal.

Always keep in mind that "human error" is a common excuse for any discrepancies. If you notice any errors, make sure to address them promptly with the PRO. Whether you or your manager is responsible, ensuring that your songs are registered without interruption is paramount.

Furthermore, if you find yourself among the top 1% of earners, you may qualify for advances from your PRO. However, this privilege is reserved for top earners, and if you do receive an advance, aim to pay it back within three quarters or less.

d) Personal Experience

Early on, I worked with a promising music producer who was excited about a project with several big-name collaborators. The music itself was solid, but I noticed he had not registered any of the songs with a PRO yet. I explained how essential it was to get his work registered, comparing it to having a license to "drive" his music career forward. After some convincing, we set him up with a particular PRO, which was the best fit for his genre and style at the time.

Soon after, a song he had worked on gained serious traction, but his royalties did not show up. When I checked, I found that the song had not been registered correctly, they called it, you guessed it, "human error." This experience taught both of us the importance of double-checking everything, no matter who is overseeing the registrations. Now, I always tell producers to stay on top of their registrations and ensure their songs are listed on the PRO's platform.

Since then, I make it a point to verify every new release is properly registered, not just with the PRO but with every organization that tracks royalties. Today, that producer I helped is in the top 1% of earners and receives regular advances from his PRO, which he pays back quickly to keep those doors open.

e) Leverage for Future Projects:

Having a stake in publishing rights not only benefits your current projects but can also enhance your leverage in future negotiations. When you can demonstrate a history of generating income through your past works, you strengthen your position in discussions with labels, artists, and other industry stakeholders. For example, consider the case of a producer who previously worked on a hit single that generated significant revenue through streams and licensing deals. This producer earned a substantial income from that track, totaling over $500,000.00 in royalties within the first year. When approaching a new label for a follow-up project, they could confidently present their history, highlighting how their previous work consistently generates revenue. This history allows them to negotiate a higher advance and a greater percentage of royalties for the new project. In negotiations, the label is likely to view the producer as an asset, increasing the chances of securing a favorable deal.

From my own experience, I remember negotiating a deal for a rising producer who had recently worked on a well-performing album. We gathered data on the album's performance—over fifteen million streams in the first month—and presented this during our discussions with a major label. By highlighting the tangible success of their previous projects, we were able to negotiate an advance that was 30% higher than the label's initial offer. This experience taught me the importance of not just relying on talent but also leveraging proven success to command respect and favorable terms in negotiations.

Moreover, market conditions can play a significant role in how leverage is perceived. For instance, if a particular streaming platform is surging in popularity, labels may be more willing to invest in producers who have demonstrated the ability to generate revenue on that platform. Staying informed about industry trends and using them to your advantage can further strengthen your negotiating position.

Ultimately, having a solid portfolio of successful works not only increases your immediate bargaining power but also lays the groundwork for a sustainable career in the music industry. By maintaining and leveraging your publishing rights, you position yourself as a key player, capable of driving projects that yield substantial returns for both you and your collaborators.

f) Impact of Song Placement

Successful placements in film, TV, or commercials can significantly enhance the value of your publishing rights. These opportunities not only lead to increased exposure but also result in higher royalty earnings, making strategic songwriting and production essential for every music creator.

For instance, consider the case of a song that gets featured in a blockbuster film. A track placed in a movie's climax can reach millions of viewers and often leads to a surge in streams and downloads post-release. When one well-known artist's song was used in a major motion picture, it saw a 300% increase in streams on platforms like Spotify and Apple Music within days of the film's premiere.

This not only generated substantial revenue from the initial placement but also ensured ongoing royalties every time the song was streamed or downloaded.

Additionally, commercials are another powerful avenue for song placements. A catchy tune featured in a popular advertisement can become ingrained in the public's mind, leading to increased sales and more streams. For example, a lesser-known artist saw their song used in a nationwide ad campaign for a soft drink. The exposure propelled their track to the top of the charts, resulting in significant royalty earnings that far exceeded what they would have received from typical album sales.

From my own experience, I collaborated with a producer who had a song featured in a popular television series. At first, it seemed like a modest placement, but within a week, we noticed a significant spike in royalties. The song's inclusion in key episodes led to a 200% increase in performance royalties that quarter. This experience highlighted the importance of actively pursuing placements and being strategic about the projects we collaborate on.

Furthermore, song placements often lead to additional opportunities, such as synchronizing licensing deals for further use in various media. Having a record of successful placements can elevate your profile, making you a sought-after collaborator for future projects. When negotiating publishing agreements or advances, you can leverage these placements to secure better terms based on your proven ability to generate income through various channels.

Ultimately, understanding the impact of song placements is crucial for producers and songwriters alike. By strategically targeting opportunities in film, TV, and commercials, you can enhance your visibility, increase your earnings, and significantly boost the overall value of your publishing rights. It is not just about creating great music; it is about creating music that fits within the larger media landscape.

g) Negotiating Publishing Agreements:

Understanding the terms of major publishing agreements is essential for maximizing your earnings as a major music producer. These agreements dictate how publishing rights are shared and can significantly impact your financial success over time.

When you contribute to a song—whether through composition, arrangement, or production—it is crucial to negotiate for an equitable share of the publishing rights. Many producers enter the industry unaware of the potential income streams tied to these rights, which can lead to undervaluing their contributions.

To effectively negotiate, consider these key points:

1. **Know the Standard Rates:**

   Familiarize yourself with industry standards for publishing shares. In many cases, lyric writers may claim 50% of the publishing rights, leaving the remaining 50%, which is typically the musical bed in the pop or hip-hop genres, for the artist and producer. If you are a key contributor, you should negotiate for a share that reflects your involvement.

2. **Highlight Your Contributions:**

   When discussing the agreement, be prepared to outline your specific contributions to the song. This can include your role in songwriting, arrangement, and production. Having a documented history of your work can strengthen your negotiating position.

3. **Be Aware of Recoupment Terms:**

   Just as with producer royalties, advances from publishing agreements are often recoupable. Understand how these terms affect your potential earnings. Be cautious of agreements that may tie up your rights for extended periods or limit your future opportunities.

4. **Engage a Lawyer:**

   Given the complexities involved in publishing agreements, having a qualified attorney can be invaluable. They can help identify favorable terms and ensure that your rights are protected. **Remember: The lawyer works for you!**

5. **Consider the Long Term:**

   A good publishing agreement not only benefits your current project but also enhances your leverage in future negotiations. Having a stake in a successful catalog can lead to better terms on subsequent projects.

Personal Experience:

During my early years in the major music business, I negotiated a publishing agreement for a talented producer I was representing. We were excited about working with a rising A-list artist whose last single had charted in the top ten.

The initial offer presented to us seemed favorable, with a 50/50 split on the exploitation of the publishing rights. However, I knew we needed to dig deeper.

As we reviewed the agreement, I noticed it included a clause that would allow the artist to retain a larger share of future earnings from sync placements and licensing opportunities. Recognizing the potential for significant revenue from these avenues, I pushed back on that clause. Through discussions, I emphasized my client's contributions to the song and how they would impact the record's commercial viability.

After several rounds of negotiation, we secured an additional 10% in publishing rights for my client, and we adjusted the sync placement clause to ensure a more equitable split. This experience was pivotal; it taught me that being well-prepared and informed is critical in negotiations. Today, my client is not only a successful producer but also a respected figure in the industry, leveraging that initial publishing deal into more lucrative agreements and collaborations.

By equipping yourself with knowledge and employing strategic negotiation techniques, you can secure agreements that reflect your true value and pave the way for future success in the music industry.

h) Collaboration and Networking:

Securing publishing rights also opens doors for collaboration with other songwriters and producers. By building a network of connections and relationships, you can create more opportunities for songwriting partnerships, leading to additional publishing income.

In summary, securing and understanding your publishing rights is a fundamental aspect of being a successful producer. Not only do these rights provide immediate financial benefits, but they also lay the groundwork for sustainable income and professional growth within the music industry. By taking the initiative-taking in managing your publishing rights, you can ensure that your contributions to music continue to pay dividends for years to come.

i) Split Sheets and Credits

Split sheets are essential documents that outline the percentage of ownership each contributor has in a song's composition. It is crucial to have these in place upfront to avoid disputes later. In the music industry, a song is typically considered to be 100%: 50% allocated to the songwriting, often referred to as the "topline," and 50% to the production side, which covers contributions toward the song lyrics, instrumentation, arrangement, and/or beat.

Just as in professional sports, where teamwork and clear roles are vital for success, the same principles apply in music production.

A current trend in the industry is the rising number of beatmakers contributing to a single track. Where two people might traditionally craft a beat, it is now common to see four or five collaborators on one beat. This dilution of ownership means that splits can end up as low as 10-12.5% per person.

Sometimes maybe these bigger groups of collaborators can be worth it. Consider, however, the way a basketball team functions: if too many players are trying to take the same shot, it can lead to confusion and missed opportunities.

Certain creative decisions can also invite more teammates. For example, if a track involves a sample, the situation can become even more complicated.

The sample clearance can take a sizable chunk of the publishing rights, sometimes halving the total available for all contributors. Given this potential, it is often better to interpolate a song rather than directly sample it, allowing for more creative control and avoiding the pitfalls of sample clearance. This is all to say that it's helpful to keep the team on the floor from getting overcrowded, leaving room for more productive teamwork.

To succeed as a beatmaker in the major music industry, it is essential to choose the right collaborators who can deliver consistent hit chemistry. Just like a successful sports team relies on players who understand each other's strengths and weaknesses, chemistry among producers and songwriters is key to creating standout tracks that resonate with audiences and generate lasting success.

j) Admin and Collection

Publishers, or administrators, play a crucial role in overseeing the collection of royalties for major music producers and songwriters, ensuring that you get paid when your music is used or performed. Signing with a reputable publisher or administrator can significantly enhance your ability to monetize your work.

There is a common misconception that you do not need a major music publisher but consider this: The major players in the major music business—Sony, UMG, and Warner—are like the top franchises in sports. To be part of a winning team, you must be accountable and deliver results.

At the same time, the idea that A&Rs, or labels are solely responsible for getting placements for music producers is a myth. While any assistance from them is a bonus, the real responsibility lies with you. Just as athletes must actively train and perform to stay in the game, major music producers need to take initiative in securing their opportunities.

Many beatmakers and loopers fall into the trap of not wanting to "get on the court." In this analogy, the recording studio is the court where the real action happens. Major music producers are in the studio every day, collaborating with artists to create timeless music. To succeed, you need to be present and engaged, consistently honing your craft, and building relationships.

NAVIGATING THE RULES: ESSENTIAL TIPS

Just as coaches provide strategies for success in the field, here are some key tips to help you navigate contracts, royalties, distribution, and publishing:

Know Your Rights:

Before signing any agreement, understand what rights you are giving up or retaining. Consult with a lawyer! Protecting your rights now prevents losses down the line.

Negotiate Everything:

Royalties, upfront fees, and distribution terms are often negotiable. Approach every contract as a chance to secure fair compensation for your work.

Document Roles and Responsibilities:

Use split sheets and maintain clear agreements with collaborators to avoid misunderstandings.

Understand Ownership vs. Licensing:

Determine if you are keeping ownership of your work or merely licensing it for use. Ownership entitles you to long-term earnings, while licensing usually provides immediate, but limited, income.

With these essential "rules of the game" in mind, you are ready to approach your career with greater clarity and confidence. Contracts, royalties, distribution, and publishing rights are the foundation of the music business, and by understanding them, you are setting yourself up to succeed in a field where knowledge truly is power.

Questions to Challenge the Reader:

1. What are the three most essential elements you should look for in a producer agreement, and why?
2. Reflect on how understanding these elements can empower you to make better business decisions when signing deals.
3. Imagine you are offered a choice between a higher upfront payment and a percentage of future royalties in a producer agreement. What factors would you consider making the best choice?
4. Think about short-term vs. long-term benefits, the artist's potential for success, and your personal financial goals.
5. If you co-write a song with an artist, what steps would you take to ensure you receive your share of the publishing rights?
6. Consider the role of split sheets, your rights as a songwriter, and how publishers might assist you in collecting royalties.
7. How does independent distribution differ from traditional label distribution, and what advantages and challenges do each present? Analyze how each distribution model could impact your control over your music, earning potential, and audience reach.
8. When reviewing a contract, what are some signs that indicate you might need a lawyer's guidance before signing?
9. Think about potential red flags like ambiguous language, unclear terms on royalties, or any ownership clauses that could impact your long-term rights.
10. What is one potential "penalty" or mistake that could arise from neglecting publishing rights, and how could you avoid it?

Reflect on the financial and career impact of not securing publishing rights and ways to prevent this outcome.

These questions are not just exercises; they are essential scenarios that will prepare you for real-world situations in the music business.

CHAPTER 2:
DEFINING ROLES ON THE TEAM

In the major music industry, just like being on a professional sports team, each person plays a unique and vital role, working together toward a shared goal: a successful project. A clear understanding of these roles—and how they collaborate—is crucial to navigating the industry and creating a winning strategy. Let us break down these positions and their functions.

KEY PLAYERS IN THE MAJOR MUSIC INDUSTRY

The Artist

Role:

The artist is the face of the music, bringing the songs to life and forging emotional connections with audiences. They embody the creative vision while building a public persona that amplifies the music's reach. However, not all artists operate on the same level, and understanding these levels is essential for navigating the industry.

Levels of Artists:

A-list Artist (Elite):

The superstar. This artist is committed to excellence and sustaining their position at the top. Comparable to an NBA starting five player who dominates the court, the A-list artist is a driving force in the industry.

Everyone wants to collaborate with this artist, because their presence can elevate your career, but only if you prove you can deliver consistent, high quality work.

B-list Artist (Seasoned):

A talented and consistent contributor, much like the dependable NBA player who ensures the team's success. While not yet a superstar, the B-list artist offers solid opportunities for growth.

Producers and songwriters should view them as a step up and treat collaborations as a platform to refine their skills and build their reputation.

C-list Artist (Emerging):

The rookie or bench player. They may show potential but often lack the ambition or ability to advance beyond the first year.

These artists might seem appealing at first, but long-term, they can hinder financial stability for producers and songwriters.

A lesson you'll learn throughout this book is to identify these artists early and focus your energy on those willing to grow and invest in their craft.

Personal experience:

Early in my career, I worked with a talented but unmotivated C-list artist. They had one breakout song, but instead of building on that success, they became complacent. My client invested countless hours in production, hoping their potential would lead to something bigger. It didn't. That experience taught us a valuable lesson: Always evaluate an artist's ambition as carefully as their talent.

Later, my client collaborated with an A-list artist who not only matched my client's energy but challenged him to push his creative limits. The result?

Multiple chart-topping hits and a lasting partnership.

THE MAJOR MUSIC PRODUCER

Role:

Many assume a producer is merely someone who lands placements with artists, but that's a limited view in 2025, when there is much more to a major producer. They are the architects of sound, responsible for crafting the overall direction and feel of a song or album. Think of the producer as a coach, guiding an artist toward their peak creative and professional performance.

Responsibilities:

A music producer oversees everything from selecting beats and arranging instruments to overseeing recording sessions and finalizing the mix. They bridge the gap between the artist's vision and the technical execution, ensuring that the final product isn't just a song, but a masterpiece that resonates with its audience. Other responsibilities include:

Collaboration:

Producers collaborate directly with artists, engineers, and sometimes label executives, aligning the creative and commercial goals of a project. It's critical to understand that the producer's role extends beyond creating beats or loops—it's about building relationships. While those who craft instrumental beats and send them via email may contribute to a song, they aren't typically remembered as producers.

Those who are present, actively collaborating in the studio, and fostering real human connections are the ones who leave a lasting impact.

Reality Check:

Too many individuals who make beats remain in their comfort zones, relying on remote submissions and virtual interactions. This industry isn't virtual, it's human. Like professional sports, where players must show up and physically compete, music production demands presence. You can't play the game from the sidelines—or your bedroom.

Practical Example:

Take Quincy Jones producing Michael Jackson's *Thriller*. While countless contributors worked on the album, Quincy's ability to guide, connect, and physically be there shaped its legendary success. His presence in the studio wasn't just about technical input—it was about leadership, vision, and trust.

Final Thought:

The music industry thrives on real relationships and collaboration. If you're comfortable staying behind a screen, you'll likely find yourself stuck. Step out. Show up. Build relationships. Remember, this is a human industry—success comes to those who are present, intentional, and committed to creating in the moment.

The Manager

Role:

A manager functions like the general manager of a sports team or an agent for a professional athlete. Their primary responsibility is to oversee the business side of a music producer's career, ensuring that the producer's creative work translates into tangible success and growth. Managers play a pivotal role in opening doors and navigating the complexities of the music industry, serving as the bridge between the creative and business worlds.

Responsibilities:

The manager's duties are multifaceted. They set up deals, negotiate contracts, and make strategic career decisions. Their role extends to identifying opportunities that align with the music producer's long-term goals while safeguarding their financial and creative interests. Managers monitor deadlines, organize schedules, and ensure that all parties involved deliver on their commitments. They also manage expectations—both producer and external collaborators, setting realistic goals and timelines that protect the producer from overextension and burnout. Other responsibilities include:

Collaboration:

Managers are the glue holding the producer's professional network together. They interact with everyone in the industry—co-producers, label executives, lawyers, and other key players—acting as the primary communicator and point of contact. A good manager keeps the producer focused on their craft by managing distractions and maintaining alignment among all collaborators.

They also serve as a sounding board, offering both business advice and emotional support when big decisions or crises arise.

Insight:

A skilled manager doesn't just manage day-to-day operations—they think long-term. They understand the trends of the industry and anticipate shifts in demand. More importantly, they nurture relationships, both old and new, to keep the producer relevant and in demand. The best managers are tech savvy, adapting to the digital age by staying up to date on social media strategies, digital distribution, and streaming platforms, which have become essential in shaping a producer's career.

Crisis Management:

A key responsibility often overlooked is crisis management. Whether it's an unexpected legal issue, a delayed project, or a problem with a collaborator, a good manager will have the experience and composure to handle these situations with professionalism and creativity. Their ability to navigate such challenges ensures the producer's career continues to flourish despite setbacks.

CASE STUDY - REAL-LIFE EXAMPLE:

A few years ago, one of my clients, Go Grizzly, faced a major challenge when a song we had been working on for months was delayed due to legal issues related to sample clearance. The label was pushing for the song's release, but the legal team was slow to finalize everything, causing a lot of stress on the project.

As Go Grizzly's manager, I immediately took charge by coordinating with the lawyers, speaking with the label to get an extension, and negotiating a fair timeline that would protect the producer's interests without sacrificing the project's momentum. I also kept Go Grizzly focused on his next projects, ensuring that he didn't lose any creative momentum. In the end, the song was released successfully, and the delay gave us the opportunity to fine-tune the track, which contributed to its success.

Pro Tip:

The best managers are those who know how to balance being assertive with being approachable. They ensure their client gets the best deal possible while fostering goodwill with other stakeholders. Producers should view their manager not just as a business partner but as someone invested in their overall success, understanding that the relationship goes beyond mere business transactions—it is a partnership built on trust, communication, and mutual respect.

The Publisher

Role:

Publishers ensure that music producers and songwriters are compensated when their work is used commercially. They manage the complex processes of licensing, royalty collection, and song promotion. However, the publishing landscape is tiered, and understanding these tiers is critical for navigating the business.

Levels of Music Publishing:

A-list Publishers:

These are the powerhouses of the industry—**Warner Chappell Music, Sony Music Publishing**, and **Universal Music Publishing Group**. These companies dominate the market, offering full-service royalty collection, global reach, and unmatched industry connections. They manage high-profile catalogs and have the resources to support large-scale marketing and promotion efforts.

A-list Administrators:

Companies like **Kobalt Music Group** provide administrative services that rival major publishers in efficiency. They specialize in royalty collection and transparency, making them a favorite among independent artists and producers seeking to maintain ownership of their work.

B-list Publishers:

These publishers often have partnerships with one or more A-list companies. They operate at a mid-level, offering decent royalty collection and song pitching services. **Winners Circle Music & Publishing** falls into this category. While they may lack the global dominance of an A-list publisher, they can provide a more personalized approach and opportunities for collaboration.

C-list Publishers:

These publishers often struggle with incomplete royalty collection services and limited industry reach. They may not have the resources or partnerships to provide full support to songwriters and producers. Collaborating with a C-list publisher can result in missed opportunities and lost income.

Responsibilities:

- **Royalty Collection:** Ensuring that all potential income streams (mechanical, performance, sync, etc.) are tracked and paid out to rights holders.
- **Licensing:** Negotiating the use of songs in films, commercials, and other media.
- **Registration:** Ensuring songs are registered with relevant performing rights organizations (PROs) and other collection agencies.
- **Song Promotion:** Pitching songs to artists, labels, and other opportunities to maximize their commercial potential.

Personal Insight:

When I first started in publishing, I worked with a small C-list publisher that promised big results. While they oversaw basic royalty collection, I discovered many streams of income were being overlooked. Switching to a B-list publisher like Winners Circle gave me access to better resources and connections, which significantly improved income streams for my clients. The real breakthrough came when I partnered with A-list administrators, which allowed my team to compete at the highest level while retaining control over our catalogs.

Key Takeaway:

Not all publishers are created equal. Understanding the distinctions between A-list, B-list, and C-list publishers can make or break your success in the music business. Partnering with the right publisher can maximize your earnings and open doors to opportunities that would otherwise remain out of reach.

The Label Executive

Role:

The key question every music producer asks is: *Which label executive can help secure a major label placement?* The truth is no one at the label is solely responsible for getting that placement. However, the individual with the most influence is often the **Head of A&R (Artists and Repertoire)**.

In the "industry standard" days, A&Rs held significant power: They scouted talent, brokered connections, and greenlit projects. Today, their influence is waning due to the dominance of the internet and social media in shaping trends. Platforms like TikTok and Instagram allow artists to bypass traditional gatekeepers, which has shifted the power dynamic.

While A&Rs still play a role, label executives, those working in the office—can be powerful allies once a producer proves their value. But remember label employees serve the company. Their loyalty lies with the label's bottom line, as their jobs depend on it.

Responsibilities:

Label executives oversee project budgets, allocate resources for marketing, and make key decisions about an artist's career trajectory. This includes financing projects, planning promotional strategies, and connecting artists with professionals like producers and songwriters.

Executives may also manage releases and coordinate with distribution channels. Their goal is to maximize the commercial success of every project under their purview.

Collaboration:

Depending on their role, executives often function as facilitators, bringing together teams of producers, artists, and marketers. They might request producers to lower their fees to meet budget constraints—a practice many producers have encountered.

Example:

Early in my career, I was asked to reduce my client's production fee for a major project to "help the budget." At first, my client agreed, thinking it would secure a long-term relationship. The project succeeded, but when the label moved to the next project, they didn't prioritize my client for the bigger opportunities. It was a harsh lesson in valuing his work and not compromising too much.

Instead of undervaluing yourself, focus on demonstrating why you're indispensable to the label. By delivering undeniable results, you position yourself as an asset they can't afford to lose.

Key Takeaway:

Label executives can be valuable partners, but they will always prioritize the company. Your best strategy is to highlight your value while standing firm on your worth. Advocate for your brand and contributions, ensuring your work is compensated fairly and your role in the success of a project is recognized.

Other Essential Roles

Two more essential creative roles are songwriters and engineers. Songwriters—that is, outside songwriters who aren't considered the primary artist on a project—compose lyrics and melodies, collaborating closely with producers and artists to craft songs that fit a project's tone. Sound engineers, mixing engineers, and mastering engineers all ensure high technical quality of the music, working under the guidance of the producer and artist.

COLLABORATION AND TEAMWORK: BRINGING IT ALL TOGETHER

In professional sports, success hinges on teamwork, with each player contributing their unique skills to achieve a common goal. In music, this concept is equally vital: Each role—from songwriters and producers to engineers and session musicians—is interdependent, and success relies on open communication, shared objectives, and mutual respect among team members.

Understanding Each Role's Contribution

Just as a basketball team thrives when the point guard effectively distributes the ball to the right players at the right time, a music producer must recognize and leverage the expertise of every collaborator. For instance, when collaborating with a vocalist, it is crucial to understand their strengths and preferences to craft arrangements that highlight their abilities.

Establishing Clear Communication

Open lines of communication are paramount. Regular check-ins during the production process can prevent misunderstandings and keep everyone aligned. For example, scheduling a pre-session meeting to outline expectations and desired outcomes can foster a collaborative atmosphere where everyone feels valued and included.

Shared Goals and Mutual Respect

Establishing shared goals is essential for a successful project. This may involve discussing the artistic vision, commercial aspirations, or even the intended audience for the music. Mutual respect ensures that every team member feels empowered to contribute ideas and feedback, creating a dynamic environment where creativity flourishes.

Personal Experience

One of my most memorable collaborations was with a diverse team on a project for a high-profile artist. Each team member played a distinct role: the songwriter crafted compelling lyrics, one producer focused on melodies, while another contributed drums and arrangement. Throughout the process, we held daily meetings to share progress, address concerns, and ensure everyone was aligned.

During one of these sessions, a conflict arose regarding the song's arrangement. Instead of dismissing differing opinions, we encouraged an open discussion. Interestingly, the artist, while not heavily involved in this aspect, trusted us to experiment. The music collaborators suggested a fresh take on the bridge, which initially seemed out of place but elevated the song. This experience reinforced the idea that respecting each other's contributions can lead to innovative outcomes that might not.

CONCLUSION

Just like in sports, where every player's contribution is vital to the team's success, in music, the collaborative spirit is what brings a project to life. By fostering a culture of open communication, mutual respect, and shared goals, producers can ensure a smoother process and a more successful project, enhancing the final product and the relationships built along the way.

QUESTIONS TO CHALLENGE THE READER:

1. **In a successful collaboration, which two roles do you think are the most crucial, and why?**
2. Consider how these roles impact the project's creative and business success.
3. **Think about the relationship between an artist and a producer. What qualities make this partnership work well, and how can misunderstandings be avoided?**
4. Reflect on the importance of communication, shared vision, and creative respect.
5. **Imagine you are the manager for a rising artist. What are three key steps you would take to build their career and protect their interests?**

Think about balancing creative goals with strategic career planning.

1. **What are some shared challenges a producer might face when collaborating with a label executive, and how could these be managed?**
2. Consider differences in creative vision, budget constraints, and expectations for commercial success.
3. **If you are an independent artist with a limited budget, which roles would you prioritize to bring on board, and why?** Weigh the potential impact of each role to get the most value from your investment.
4. **How do you assess an artist's level and potential for growth before committing to a project?**
5. **Have you worked with a C-list artist before? What were the challenges, and what did you learn from the experience?**
6. **What steps can you take to position yourself to work with more A-list artists in the future?**

CHAPTER 3:
THE MAJOR MUSIC PRODUCER'S ROLE

In the dynamic world of major music production, the role of the 'major music producer' is both pivotal and multifaceted. This term refers to producers who operate within the high-end, major-label segment of the music industry, akin to top-tier athletes in the NBA, as opposed to those working at the high school or college level of the business. These producers are the architects behind the scenes, shaping the sound, direction, and overall quality of a musical project. For anyone looking to navigate this higher level of the industry, understanding what a producer does, the distinctions between various types of producers, and the varied responsibilities they hold is essential.

WHAT DOES A MAJOR MUSIC PRODUCER DO?

A major music producer wears many hats, acting as a blend of creative visionary, technical expert, and project manager. Their influence spans from the initial conception of a track to its final polish, ensuring that the artist's vision is realized while maintaining commercial viability.

Key Responsibilities:

1. Creative Direction:

a) Shaping the Sound:

Producers collaborate with artists to develop the unique sound of a track or album. They help artists refine their ideas and explore different sonic possibilities.

b) Songwriting and Arrangement:

While not always songwriters themselves, major music producers often contribute to the songwriting process, helping to structure songs for maximum impact. This includes decisions on song form, transitions, and instrumental choices.

2. Technical Expertise:

a) Recording Oversight:

Producers oversee recording sessions, ensuring each take meets the desired quality. They work closely with sound engineers, which requires a deep understanding of the recording equipment and techniques.

b) Mixing and Mastering:

Although some major music producers specialize in these areas, many coordinate with mixing and mastering engineers to finalize the sound of a track. The producer's role here is to ensure that the final product is polished and ready for distribution.

3. Project Management:

a) Budgeting:

Some major music producers manage the financial aspects of a project, ensuring it stays within budget while achieving high-quality results, like how a general manager oversees a team's salary cap. They must negotiate costs for studio time, musicians, and other resources effectively.

b) Scheduling:

Producers should coordinate timelines, making sure recording sessions, revisions, and releases happen on schedule—just as coach plans practices and game schedules. This involves collaborating closely with all stakeholders to align their schedules.

4. Collaboration and Communication:

a) Team Coordination:

Producers function as the central hub, communicating between artists, engineers, label executives, and other stakeholders to keep the project cohesive, akin to how a team captain facilitates communication on the field. They must ensure everyone is on the same page regarding goals and expectations.

b) Conflict Resolution:

Producers also mediate any creative differences that arise, ensuring that the project stays on track without compromising artistic integrity—much like a coach resolving player disputes to maintain team harmony. The ability to balance artistic vision with practical constraints is crucial for a successful producer.

Types of Producers

In the world of the major music labels, there are several types of producers, each serving unique roles within the production process:

1. **Executive Producer:**

   This producer oversees the entire project, making high-level decisions about budget, timelines, and overall direction. They often have a hand in selecting the creative team and ensuring that the project aligns with the label's goals.

2. **Recording Producer:**

   Often the most direct, the recording producer collaborates closely with artists during the recording sessions, guiding performances and making real-time decisions about sound and arrangements.

3. **Mixing Engineer:**

   While not always classified as a producer, mixing engineers play a critical role in shaping the final sound of a recording. They focus on blending the various elements of a track, ensuring clarity, balance, and impact.

4. **Beatmaker or Track Producer:**

   These producers specialize in creating beats or instrumental tracks, particularly in genres like hip-hop and electronic music. They often collaborate closely with artists to develop unique sounds that drive the project.

Major Producers vs. Beatmakers

While all producers play a crucial role in music creation, there are distinct differences between major producers and those who specialize as beatmakers. Understanding these distinctions can help aspiring producers identify their niche and develop the necessary skills for their chosen path.

We've already covered the producers' responsibilities. Beatmakers specialize in creating specific instrumental tracks, beats, or loops—like how a wide receiver specializes in catching passes. For example, a beatmaker/looper might make a guitar loop, violin loop, or the snare drum base pattern, for an example, often using digital audio workstations (DAWs), in which many of them are highly skilled. Beatmakers frequently then sell these beats to artists, providing an essential musical backdrop, forming the backbone of many songs, particularly in hip-hop and electronic music. And by offering pre-made beats, they make it easier for artists to produce music without needing to compose every element from scratch. Their task is more technical and granular than the broader-based producer.

A couple of well-known beatmakers include TurnMeUpJosh, whose work has become synonymous with contemporary rap, and Yak Beats, who is also a major producer—but has significantly influenced new wave hip-hop with his beat making.

Major Music Producers

Role and Responsibilities:

a) Comprehensive Oversight:

Major producers manage the entire production process from start to finish, like a head coach overseeing all aspects of team performance.

b) Creative Visionaries:

These producers often have a signature sound or style, influencing the artistic direction of the music, like how a coach's philosophy shapes a team's playing style.

c) Industry Connections:

Major producers typically have extensive networks within the music industry, which can open doors to high-profile collaborations—just as a successful coach's connection can lead to better recruitment and sponsorships.

Significance:

a) Shaping Careers:

Major producers can significantly impact an artist's career, crafting hits that resonate with audiences and gain widespread acclaim, much like a coach who elevates players to new heights.

b) Trend Setting:

Their innovative approaches often set trends within the industry, influencing the sound and direction of contemporary music, like how successful strategies in football can inspire other teams.

Examples:

- **Pooh Beatz:** Known for crafting numerous pop hits, his influence on modern hip hop is profound.
- **Smash David:** Renowned for his versatility across genres, he has left a lasting mark on artists from Khalid to Bad Bunny.
- **Go Grizzly:** his contributions as a major music producer have significantly influenced hip hop, pop, and R&B music.

CONCLUSION

The role of the producer is integral to the success of any musical project. Whether serving as a major producer overseeing every aspect of production or specializing as a beatmaker providing foundational elements, producers shape the sound and direction of the music industry. Understanding the distinct types of producers and their responsibilities allows aspiring professionals to identify their niche, develop relevant skills, and collaborate effectively within the industry's ecosystem like how a successful football team functions best when each player understands their role and works toward a common goal.

Questions to Challenge the Reader:

1. **Understanding Your Unique Value**

   What specific skills or qualities make you stand out as a major music producer? How can you communicate effectively with artists, labels, and collaborators?

2. **Adapting to Industry Expectations**

   How well do you understand the expectations that come with working at the major music level? What areas do you feel confident in, and where could you improve?

3. **Balancing Creativity with Business**

   How do you strike a balance between your creative work and the business side of your role? Are there areas where you feel one tends to overshadow the other?

4. **Defining Your Team's Contributions**

   Who are the essential team members you rely on to bring a project to life? How do you ensure that everyone's role is clear, and that each person is maximizing their strengths?

5. **Building Strong Relationships**

   How would you rate your current network and professional relationships? What steps can you take to strengthen relationships that could elevate your position in the industry?

6. **Overseeing High-Stakes Projects**

   When faced with a high-stakes project, what strategies do you employ to manage pressure and deliver your best work? Are there specific methods that help you stay focused?

7. **Evaluating Opportunities**

   How do you determine which projects align with your long-term goals as a major music producer? Are there criteria you use to decide whether an opportunity is worth pursuing?

8. **Maintaining Your Creative Vision**

   How do you preserve your creative vision while meeting commercial demands? Do you have examples where you successfully balanced these, or times when it was a struggle?

9. **Setting Standards for Your Work**

   What standards do you set for yourself and your projects to ensure that each one reflects your best work? How do these standards impact your reputation?

10. **Reflecting on Your Role Evolution**

    How has your understanding of a major music producer's role evolved as you have gained experience? What insights have helped you refine your approach and grow in the industry?

11. **Have you evaluated whether your current publisher provides full royalty collection services?**

12. How can you position yourself to work with an A-list publisher or administrator in the future?

13. What steps can you take to ensure all your songs are properly registered and earn their full potential?

CHAPTER 4:
ASSEMBLING YOUR
MUSIC INDUSTRY TEAM

In the major-label world, success as a producer requires more than just talent. It's built on strategic collaborations with skilled professionals who help bring your projects to life and amplify your reach. Each person in your music team plays a part in moving your career forward. This chapter explores the key industry players every major music producer should know, their specific roles, and strategies for building a network that drives your success.

BUILDING A POWERFUL TEAM IN THE MAJOR MUSIC INDUSTRY

As a music producer, having the right support network is crucial to navigating the complexities of high-profile projects, major label expectations, and audience demands. Below are essential collaborators who help propel your career forward and ensure that every project reaches its highest potential:

THE MAJOR-LABEL MUSIC PRODUCER MANAGER:

Role, Responsibilities, and Value

In the major-label world, the role of a producer manager is essential for a producer's long-term success. This person serves as the producer's advocate and guide, ensuring they are positioned for the best opportunities while allowing them to focus on the creative side of their work.

Just as artists have managers who shape their careers, a skilled producer manager helps producers navigate the business landscape, secure high-level collaborations, and achieve significant career milestones.

Key Responsibilities of a Major Music Producer Manager:

1. Career Strategy and Development

a) Long-Term Planning:

A Major Music Producer Manager collaborates with you to set career goals, identifying key milestones like collaborations, brand partnerships, and significant projects that align with your vision. Much like a coach maps out a season's strategy, a manager ensures that your trajectory in the industry is well-defined.

b) Skill Development:

Managers can also advise on areas of growth needed, helping you stay competitive with changing industry standards and encouraging you to build skills that align with your goals. They help you identify workshops, courses, and opportunities that can enhance your craft.

2. Negotiation

a) Securing Contracts:

Major Music Producer Managers negotiate contracts with labels, artists, and publishing companies. Their expertise ensures that the terms are fair, compensation is optimal, and your rights are protected. Just as Pat Riley secured favorable contracts for his players, a Major Music Producer Manager fights for the best terms on your behalf.

b) Protecting Royalties:

Managers pay close attention to royalty splits, ensuring you receive ongoing revenue from your contributions. This vigilance is essential in a complex industry where income can come from various streams.

3. Financial Oversight

a) Revenue Management:

Managers help you track income, from advances to royalty payments, ensuring you receive what you are owed and helping you plan future projects. Like a team's financial manager, they keep a close eye on your earnings and expenditure, making sure you remain financially healthy.

4. Networking and Building Relationships

a) Industry Connections:

A manager leverages their network to connect you with artists, labels, and other producers who can elevate your career. They are the bridge to opportunities that may not be accessible without strong industry ties.

b) Strategic Collaborations:

By introducing you to collaborators whose work complements yours, managers help you gain more exposure and expand your creative range. They understand the power of collaboration and work to align you with like-minded creatives.

The Difference Between "Major" Music Producer Managers and Music Producer Managers

Understanding what distinguishes a major music producer manager and a regular music producer manager is crucial for navigating the music industry landscape effectively. Both roles involve managing producers, but they operate at different levels of the industry with varying degrees of influence and expertise.

First, a major music producer manager is a seasoned professional with a proven record in the major music business. They typically manage clients who are signed to major publishing companies and are actively engaged in high profile projects. They possess extensive industry connections, negotiate significant contracts, and strategize long-term career paths for their clients.

In other words, they have established relationships with major players in the industry, including record labels, publishers, and other influential figures. They understand the nuances of the business at a prominent level and can navigate complex negotiations effectively.

On the other hand, a non-major music producer manager may operate at a lower-profile level, managing producers who might not yet be signed to major publishers or who are still building their careers. They may not have the same depth of industry connections, and often work with emerging talent, focusing on skill development and gaining exposure. These managers help guide their clients through the initial stages of their careers, offering support and guidance as they grow.

There's a lot of value in working with a major music producer manager. They can oversee business concerns, allowing you to focus on creative output and innovation. This partnership fosters career longevity, creating a support system that allows you to maximize both creative fulfillment and financial success.

TIPS FOR CHOOSING THE RIGHT MAJOR MUSIC PRODUCER MANAGER

1. **Alignment with Your Vision:**

   Look for a manager who understands your long-term goals and shares your values and vision for your career.

2. **Industry Connections:**

   Choose someone with a well-established network within the major music industry, who can open doors to high-profile projects.

3. **Experience with Royalties and Rights:**

   Your manager should understand royalty structures, intellectual property rights, and contractual terms specific to producers.

4. **Transparent Communication:**

   Good managers are communicative, keeping you informed and updated about every stage of a project, from negotiation to completion.

Label Executive

Role and Responsibilities:

1. **Project Funding and Resources:**

   Label executives oversee budgets for recording, marketing, and distribution, ensuring that each project has the resources it needs to succeed.

2. **Strategic Guidance:**

   They play a vital role in positioning and distributing music, as well as offering career advice and support.

3. **Distribution and Reach:**

   Labels oversee the planning of releasing music on streaming platforms and within international markets, helping producers reach wider audiences.

Importance:

- Label executives provide the funding, influence, and industry reach that make large-scale projects possible, opening doors to significant growth.

Building a Strong Relationship:

- Foster open communication and respect with label executives. A collaborative relationship ensures that your projects align with both creative and commercial goals.

Music Publisher

Role and Responsibilities:

a) Rights Management and Royalties:

Publishers ensure your music is properly registered, royalties are collected, and licenses are managed efficiently.

b) Promotion and Placements:

They actively seek placements in films, TV shows, ads, and other media to maximize your song's visibility and earnings.

c) Songwriting Opportunities:

Publishers often facilitate collaborations with other writers and producers, expanding your network and creative possibilities.

Importance:

- Publishers are essential in helping producers and artists protect their intellectual property and maximize the revenue potential of each track.

Building a Strong Relationship:

- Work with publishers who understand your goals and actively seek opportunities that align with your vision. Collaboration with a publisher who takes initiative can lead to valuable placements and increased exposure.

Legal and Financial Advisors

Role and Responsibilities:

a) Contract Negotiation:

Lawyers protect your interests in every contract, from label deals to sync licenses, ensuring you are well-compensated, and your rights are intact.

b) Financial Planning:

Accountants manage finances, taxes, and budgets, helping you sustain and grow your wealth.

c) Intellectual Property Protection:

Legal advisors ensure your rights are protected across multiple markets and platforms, safeguarding your future earnings.

Importance:

- Advisors protect your long-term interests and financial well-being, allowing you to focus on creating music with peace of mind.

Building a Strong Relationship:

- Choose advisors with experience in the major music industry. Their understanding of high stakes deals and royalties will be invaluable in securing your success.

STRATEGIES FOR EFFECTIVE NETWORKING IN THE MAJOR MUSIC INDUSTRY

To put a team together, you need to put yourself out there and network. Here are some strategies to keep in mind.

1. **Attend Exclusive Industry Events:**

   Participate in conferences, awards, and festivals that attract top producers, executives, and artists. These events offer networking with key industry influencers who can open doors to new collaborations.

2. **Leverage social media with Intent:**

   Social platforms allow you to share your work, connect with fans, and engage with industry leaders. Comment on the work of others, highlight your expertise, and establish yourself as a knowledgeable professional in your field.

3. **Collaboration on High-Impact Projects:**

   Work on projects with other well-known artists or producers to expand your influence and reach. Collaborative projects often yield new networking opportunities and boost your visibility.

4. **Seek Out Mentors and Advisors:**

   Mentorship from experienced industry figures can offer insights and open doors to valuable connections. Do not hesitate to ask for guidance and stay proactive in maintaining those relationships.

Always Follow Up:

After an initial meeting, follow up with a thoughtful message expressing your interest in staying connected—even if there isn't an immediate project to work on. Building and nurturing relationships over time can lead to future collaborations.

The Importance of Relationships and Teamwork for Major Producers

A powerful network of industry professionals forms the backbone of a producer's career. Strong relationships help you gain exposure, navigate industry challenges, and maintain momentum as you reach new career heights. Collaborating with a team that shares your vision and values ensures that each project meets the highest standards and achieves optimal success.

Questions to Challenge the Reader:

1. **What qualities would you prioritize in a producer manager, and why?**

   Think about the specific skills, experience, and connections that would best support your career goals.

2. **How can a manager help you achieve a better work-life balance as a producer?**

   Reflect on how having a manager manage schedules and negotiations could allow you to focus more on creativity.

3. **What are the potential challenges of collaborating with a producer manager, and how would you address them?**

   Consider how to maintain open communication, manage expectations, and ensure mutual respect in the relationship.

   By selecting the right major music manager and establishing a clear partnership, you can better navigate the complex world of the major music industry, build your brand, and achieve sustained success.

   These questions encourage you to assess the importance of teamwork, understand the impact of industry relationships, and build a network that aligns with your ambitions as a major music producer.

CHAPTER 5:
THE CREATIVE PROCESS
FROM CONCEPT TO COMPLETION

Producing music is like building a championship-winning team in professional sports. Each step in production—from initial brainstorming to final mastering—demands precision, teamwork, and creativity. Just as a coach guides a team to victory, a producer guides the creative and technical process to achieve a powerful, polished track.

THE STEPS OF MUSIC PRODUCTION: FROM PRE-GAME TO POST-GAME

1. Pre-Production: The Playbook and Game Plan

Conceptualization:

Just as coaches strategize based on the opponent's strengths and weaknesses, producers start by establishing the concept for the song or album. What is the intended mood, genre, or message? Like a game plan, this phase sets the vision.

Songwriting and Arrangement:

This is like drawing up plays, figuring out how each player (or instrument) will contribute. Song structure, tempo, and arrangement become the "game positions," defining how the elements will work together.

Budgeting and Planning:

In major league sports, every team has a budget, and so does every music project. Producers "budget their cap space," allocating funds for studio time, musicians, and other resources, ensuring the project does not run out of resources mid-season.

2. Tracking: The Team on the Field

Recording Instruments and Vocals:

In the performance phase, every musician and vocalist record their parts, aiming for excellence. Every instrument and vocal track adds to a song's power.

Session Musicians:

Sometimes producers bring in session musicians of particularly strong experience to add their expertise and quality to the track.

Vocal Direction:

Producers coach vocalists to achieve the best outcome, like a coach guiding a player to get the perfect shot. With constructive feedback, the producer ensures the artist reaches their peak performance.

3. Editing: Reviewing the Game Footage

Refining Tracks:

In this stage, producers work on each track to refine and perfect it, cutting unnecessary parts, and piecing together the best parts of each take. Everything must align seamlessly, just as a team operates best when every player is in sync—only in music, you can go back and make changes, rather than relying solely on the initial outcome.

Sound Quality Enhancement:

Every detail counts, from pitch and timing to the elimination of background noise. Producers fine-tune every sound to achieve flawless performance.

4. Mixing: Building Team Chemistry

Balancing Elements:

During the mixing process, the producer balances each track's volume, EQ, and dynamics, creating a cohesive, dynamic sound.

Depth and Dynamics:

Much like positioning players on the field, mixing involves placing instruments and effects to create a sense of depth and space. This adds emotional impact, giving the song life and movement.

Final Adjustments:

This phase covers any small tweaks at the end of the process, which can make a significant difference to ensure a strong, impactful outcome.

5. Mastering: The Final Touchdown

Polishing the Sound:

Mastering is the last step. This process enhances the track's clarity, consistency, and punch, making it ready for any "arena" or listening environment.

Preparing for Distribution:

In sports, teams are prepped for all conditions, weather, crowds, and locations. Similarly, mastering ensures that the track sounds polished and balanced across all listening devices.

6. Feedback and Final Adjustments: Post-Game Analysis

Team Review:

Like watching and learning from a game replay, feedback helps to ensure the track is at its best. Producers often seek feedback from collaborators or even small test audiences before a final release.

FINAL CHANGES:

Based on feedback, producers may make slight changes, just as a team tweaks its game plan before the next match, ensuring the track hits every intended mark.

Fostering Creativity and Innovation: Building Team Morale and Strategy

1. **Creating the Right Atmosphere**

   The studio environment is like the locker room where trust, motivation, and focus are built, and it's up to the producer to set that tone and build that trust. A comfortable, inspiring environment helps musicians and vocalists perform at their best. A team also needs to believe in each other; by respecting each artist's input and offering constructive feedback, producers build morale that fuels creativity.

2. **Encouraging Experimentation: Trying New Plays**

   Just as sports teams innovate with new plays, producers push for new sounds, approaches, and techniques. Encouraging artists to try fresh ideas often leads to creative breakthroughs that set the track apart. This can include collaborative brainstorming; inviting team input opens possibilities for creative additions and enhances the overall result.

3. **Managing Creative Blocks: Calling Timeouts**

   When creativity hits a wall, taking a break can reset the team's energy. Stepping away, working on a different part of the track, or even changing the setup can inspire fresh ideas. Also, be sure to offer plenty of encouragement; artists need motivation as much as athletes or any other high-pressure performers. Words of encouragement and reminders of past successes keep everyone inspired and focused.

4. **Leveraging Technology: Using Advanced Training Tools**

   Just as sports teams use advanced technology for training, producers can enhance creativity with new production tools. From virtual instruments to sound manipulation software, these tools add new layers to the track. Experimenting with unique sounds or sampled elements can add the "signature move" that makes a track memorable.

QUESTIONS TO CHALLENGE THE READER:

1. What is your "game plan" in the studio? How do you approach each step to ensure success from the first take to the final mix?
2. How do you coach others in the studio environment? What are your techniques for bringing out the best in each team member?
3. When faced with creative blocks, what "timeouts" do you take to refresh your ideas?
4. How do you evaluate the track's readiness? What qualities make a track feel "championship-ready" for release?

With a clear game plan, dedicated team chemistry, and the right environment, producers can create a path to musical success that rivals the thrill and discipline of any major sport.

CHAPTER 6:
MARKETING AND BRANDING

BUILDING YOUR BRAND AS A MUSIC PRODUCER

In the highly competitive music industry, a producer's brand is paramount to their success. Your brand is not just your name; it is your reputation, your unique style, and how you are perceived in the marketplace. Just as athletes and other public figures develop personal brands that resonate with fans and sponsors, music producers must strategically cultivate their identities to attract artists, labels, and listeners.

1. Defining Your Brand Identity

Unique Selling Proposition (USP):

Start by identifying what makes you different from other producers. This could be a signature sound, expertise in a particular genre, or innovative production techniques. For example, if you specialize in blending electronic elements with classical instruments, that becomes your USP. Create a tagline or mission statement that encapsulates this identity, much like an athlete might have a personal motto.

Visual and Auditory Elements:

Your visual branding—logos, color schemes, and graphics—should be cohesive and reflective of your music style. Think about branding like a sports team: the logo, uniforms, and merchandise all represent the team's identity. Additionally, consider developing an auditory brand—signature sounds or styles that listeners associate with your productions.

2. Creating a Strong Online Presence

Website and Portfolio:

Your website serves as your digital business card. Include high-quality content that highlights your best work. Create a portfolio that highlights key projects, including tracks, album credits, and testimonials from artists. You can also feature a blog where you share insights about the production process, industry trends, or individual experiences, establishing yourself as a thought leader in the field.

Social Media Engagement:

Use platforms like Instagram, YouTube, X, TikTok, and LinkedIn to connect with your audience. Share engaging content such as behind-the scenes videos, production tips, and personal stories. Collaborate with artists and share their content to broaden your reach. Remember, social media is a two-way street; engaging with followers by responding to comments and messages fosters a sense of community.

3. Networking and Relationship-Building

Industry Connections:

Just as athletes rely on their coaches and trainers, producers need to build a network of industry contacts. Attend music festivals, workshops, and conferences to meet key players. Use platforms like LinkedIn to connect with industry professionals. Follow up new connections to establish ongoing relationships—much like a sports team building chemistry over time.

Collaborative Projects:

Collaborating with artists, other producers, and songwriters can enhance your portfolio and credibility. For example, co-producing a track with a well-known artist can expose you to their fanbase. Approach collaborations with a mindset of mutual benefit, akin to teammates working together to achieve a common goal. **4.** Promotional Strategies

Releases and Campaigns:

When planning a release, create a marketing campaign that builds anticipation. Consider how sports teams promote their games, or how movie studios promote an upcoming blockbuster; use teasers, countdowns, and exclusive previews to generate excitement. Implement a launch strategy that includes social media blasts, email newsletters, and even live listening events.

Visual Content:

High-quality videos can serve as powerful promotional tools. They help convey the story behind a song and visually represent your brand. Investing in a professional video, akin to a team creating a highlight reel, can significantly enhance your exposure and attract new listeners.

5. Leveraging Digital Platforms

Streaming Services and Playlists:

Familiarize yourself with platforms like Spotify, Apple Music, and SoundCloud. Understand the importance of playlist placements and how to pitch your music to curators.

Create your own playlists featuring your work alongside other artists to increase visibility, like how sports highlights package performances for wider audiences.

Using Data Analytics:

Utilize analytics tools provided by digital platforms to track engagement, audience demographics, and listening habits. Understanding your audience is crucial for tailoring your marketing efforts. For example, if you notice a spike in streams from a specific region, consider targeting your promotional efforts there—just as a sports team adjusts their strategy based on opponent weaknesses.

6. Building a Lasting Reputation

Consistency and Professionalism:

Maintain a prominent level of professionalism in all your interactions. Deliver on promises, meet deadlines, and communicate clearly. Reputation is everything in the music industry; much like an athlete's career hinges on their performance and conduct, producers must build a trustworthy brand to secure ongoing opportunities.

Continuous Learning and Adaptation:

The major music industry is constantly evolving. Stay informed about the latest trends, technologies, and marketing strategies. Attend workshops, take online courses, and follow industry news. Adaptation is key to staying relevant, much like athletes continuously refining their skills and strategies to outperform their competition.

CONCLUSION: CREATING YOUR LEGACY

By mastering the principles of marketing and branding, music producers can carve out their niche in the industry and create a legacy that resonates with artists and fans alike. A strong brand not only enhances visibility but also fosters trust and respect, leading to lasting collaborations and success.

QUESTIONS TO CHALLENGE THE READER:

1. What specific elements of your brand identity can you develop further to distinguish yourself in the music industry?
2. How can you enhance your online presence to attract more collaborators and clients?
3. What networking strategies will you implement to build meaningful relationships within the industry?
4. Describe a successful promotional campaign you have experienced or studied. What elements made it effective, and how can you apply those strategies to your own work?
5. In what ways can data analytics inform your marketing strategies and help you understand your audience better?

CHAPTER 7:
NAVIGATING CHALLENGES

In the fast-paced and ever-evolving landscape of the major music labels, producers face a myriad of challenges that can impact their careers and creative output. Producers must be equipped to navigate these hurdles effectively. This chapter delves into some common pitfalls and provides actionable strategies to maintain professionalism and succeed in the face of adversity.

SIGNING UNFAVORABLE CONTRACTS

One of the most significant risks for producers is entering into contracts that may not be in the best interest. This includes clauses related to royalties, ownership rights, and the duration of agreements. Many producers may not fully understand the legal language, leading to agreements that can be restrictive or detrimental. In professional sports, athletes often face similar challenges when signing contracts, where terms can favor the team over the player, especially if the player lacks experience or proper representation.

NAVIGATING THE COMPETITIVE LANDSCAPE

One reason I've used so many sports metaphors throughout this book is that the music industry can be just as competitive as professional sports, with new talent emerging constantly. Producers must find ways to stay relevant and continually evolve their sound and approach. One vital task is to stay updated on emerging trends – not just passing fads, but also genuine innovations. This might involve experimenting with new genres, collaborating with diverse artists, or adopting modern technologies.

Maintaining relevance also means building a dedicated team and being open to collaboration. For producers, building a reliable network of collaborators, including songwriters, musicians, and sound engineers, is crucial. Producers must also collaborate closely with artists and their teams to create cohesive projects. This collaboration can enhance creativity and lead to more successful outcomes.

FINANCIAL (MIS)MANAGEMENT

Producers must also be savvy with their finances. Many major music producers experience fluctuations in income due to the project-based nature of their work. Producers need to familiarize themselves with the different revenue streams available, such as royalties, advances, and licensing fees, like how athletes navigate their salaries and endorsements. This understanding helps them plan for the long term and avoid financial pitfalls.

Financial literacy is key, because many producers are creative individuals who may not have extensive training in financial management. This can result in poor budgeting, failure to track income and expenses, mismanaging revenue, and general financial instability. For example, a successful producer might spend lavishly on equipment and studio space without considering the long-term sustainability of their income, leading to cash flow issues.

NEGLECTING RELATIONSHIPS

In the music industry, relationships are key. Failing to cultivate and maintain professional connections can hinder a producer's ability to secure projects, collaborate with artists, and gain referrals. A producer who works in isolation will miss opportunities that arise through word-of-mouth and personal connections. This is a fact.

STRATEGIES FOR OVERCOMING CHALLENGES

Luckily, each of these potential pitfalls has strategies that can help you avoid major mistakes:

1. **Educate Yourself on Contracts:** Before signing any agreement, consult with a lawyer specializing in entertainment law. They can help clarify the terms and ensure you are protected. Also, numerous online resources and courses focus on music contracts and rights. Investing time in understanding these concepts will empower you to make informed decisions.

2. **Stay Informed about Industry Trends:** Subscribe to music industry publications, podcasts, and blogs to stay updated on trends, modern technologies, and changing audience preferences. Awareness of the market landscape is crucial for staying relevant— as is openness to trying new production techniques, genres, and tools. Experimentation can lead to innovation, helping you stand out in a crowded market.

3. **Implement Financial Management Practices:** Establish a budget that tracks all income and expenses related to your music production work. Use software tools or apps designed for budgeting to simplify this process. You also can and should work with a financial advisor who understands the music industry, and who can help you develop a sustainable financial plan. This allows you to invest wisely and save for future projects.

4. **Foster Networking Skills:** Make it a point to attend music festivals, conferences, and workshops where you can meet industry professionals. Networking is akin to a sports team building chemistry; it requires time and effort. You should also use platforms like LinkedIn, Instagram, and Twitter to connect with other industry players. Engage with their content and participate in discussions to establish rapport.

MAINTAINING PROFESSIONALISM

One technique that helps overcome a wide variety of potential challenges and helps you maintain a sense of professionalism in the industry is transparent communication. Always maintain open lines of communication with artists, managers, and collaborators. Clear communication helps set expectations and avoids misunderstandings. Another aspect of professionalism is the ability to adapt to challenges and bounce back from setbacks, rather than letting them overcome you. View obstacles as opportunities for learning and development, not anger, frustration, or blame.

CONCLUSION: BUILDING A RESILIENT CAREER

Navigating challenges in the music industry requires a proactive approach and a willingness to learn. By understanding common pitfalls and implementing effective strategies, producers can maintain professionalism and build successful, sustainable careers. Much like athletes, the ability to overcome adversity can define your legacy in the major music business.

Questions to Challenge the Reader:

1. Reflect on the time you faced a challenge in your music career. What did you learn from that experience, and how can you apply those lessons moving forward?
2. How can you enhance your understanding of contracts to ensure you are making informed decisions in future agreements?
3. What steps will you take to improve your financial management skills and ensure the sustainability of your career?
4. Identify three key industry contacts you would like to connect with. What is your plan to reach out to them?
5. How do you stay informed about changes in the music industry, and what resources can you utilize to further enhance your knowledge?

CHAPTER 8:
DEVELOPING A WINNING MINDSET

In the competitive arena of the music industry, success is often dictated not only by talent and skill but also by the mindset of the individuals involved. Much like athletes who must maintain focus and perseverance, music producers face challenges that require a strategic and resilient approach. This chapter dives into the essential qualities of a winning mindset, emphasizing resilience, adaptability, and professionalism as critical factors for navigating the complexities of the major music business.

ASPECTS OF A STRATEGIC MINDSET

1. Setting Clear Goals:

Just as athletes set specific performance goals—such as improving their shooting percentage or achieving a personal best—music producers must define clear, actionable objectives for their careers. Whether it is producing a certain number of tracks, collaborating with specific artists, or achieving financial milestones, having well-defined goals provides direction and motivation. These goals should be accompanied by measurable outcomes, so you can track your progress, like how athletes might monitor their performance stats. This could involve tracking the number of placements, income from royalties, or social media engagement.

Regularly assessing your achievements can help refine your strategies and maintain focus.

2. A Growth Mindset: Embracing Challenges and Continuous Learning

A growth mindset involves viewing challenges as opportunities for growth rather than obstacles. Much like athletes who learn from losses to improve their game, producers should embrace the learning process and be open to feedback, even if it feels uncomfortable. This adaptability can lead to greater creativity and innovation in your work. Stay curious and committed to expanding your knowledge and skills. Consider taking workshops, online courses, and seeking mentorship to ensure you remain relevant and informed.

3. Resilience: Overcoming Rejection, Managing Stress, and Maintaining Motivation

Working in the music industry, rejection is inevitable—whether it's a rejected pitch for a song or an artist choosing another producer. Instead of allowing rejection to demoralize you, use it as a learning experience, much like an athlete reviewing game tape after a loss. Analyze what went wrong and adjust your approach for the next opportunity. Stay motivated by focusing on your passion for music. Just as athletes lean on their training and support systems during tough times, surround yourself with a supportive network that encourages you.

Remember, persistence is key; many successful producers faced numerous rejections before finding their breakthrough.

The pressure of these types of rejections, as well as various deadlines, client expectations, and creative blocks can lead to stress. Develop healthy coping mechanisms, such as exercise, meditation, or hobbies outside of music, to help manage stress and maintain mental well-being—like how athletes engage in physical training and mental conditioning to manage pressure. Strive for a work-life balance that allows for creativity without burnout. Just as athletes must rest to recover, taking breaks and allowing yourself time to recharge can lead to greater productivity and inspiration in your work.

4. Adaptability: Embracing Change:

The major music industry is subject to rapid changes, from shifts in musical genres to advancements in technology. Producers, like athletes adjusting their training regimens based on their sport's evolving landscape, must be willing to adapt their strategies to stay relevant. Stay attuned to market trends and be prepared to pivot your approach accordingly. Do not be afraid to experiment with new sounds, production techniques, and collaborations. Embracing innovation can lead to fresh ideas and unique projects that resonate with audiences, like how athletes try new plays or techniques to stay ahead of their competition.

Part of adaptability depends on your ability to build and maintain relationships with industry professionals, including artists, managers, and label executives. Networking is not just about making contacts; it is about cultivating genuine relationships that can lead to future opportunities.

Be sure to approach every interaction with professionalism, regardless of the outcome. Just as athletes must conduct themselves with integrity on and off the field, how you manage relationships and conduct business can influence your reputation in the industry. Always be respectful, punctual, and prepared.

5. Professionalism

Consistently deliver high-quality work on time and follow through on commitments. Your reliability builds trust with collaborators and clients, enhancing your professional reputation, like how an athlete's consistency can secure their place on a team. You must also uphold ethical standards in all your dealings.

This applies to negotiating contracts—an area where many might be tempted to cut corners. Before entering any negotiation, do your homework. Understand the market value of your work, know your worth, and be prepared to articulate your position clearly.

This preparation builds confidence and empowers you to advocate for yourself effectively. Approach negotiations with a mindset of collaboration rather than confrontation. Aim for win-win solutions that benefit all parties involved.

Whether negotiating contracts or collaborating with artists, integrity is paramount. Just as athletes are expected to play fair, being known for your professionalism and ethical conduct can set you apart in a competitive industry.

CONCLUSION: BUILDING A LEGACY THROUGH MINDSET

Developing a winning mindset is essential for thriving in the music industry. By cultivating resilience, adaptability, and professionalism, music producers can navigate challenges and seize opportunities with confidence. As you continue your journey in the major music business, remember that your mindset shapes your experiences and defines your legacy—just as it does for athletes striving for greatness.

Questions to Challenge the Reader:

1. Reflect on a recent setback in your career. What strategies did you use to overcome it, and what lessons did you learn?
2. What specific goals do you want to achieve in the next year? Outline actionable steps to reach those goals.
3. How do you currently manage stress related to your work? Are there additional strategies you could incorporate to maintain balance?
4. Identify a recent trend in the music industry that interests you. How can you adapt your work to align with this trend?
5. What negotiation tactics have you used in the past, and how can you refine your approach to achieve better outcomes?

CHAPTER 9:
CHAMPIONSHIP STORIES

In any field, past success leaves clues. In the music industry, where the path to success can often seem elusive, studying the journeys of those who have made their mark can provide invaluable insights. This chapter presents a collection of championship stories from successful artists, producers, and managers. Each story illustrates the unique strategies and mindsets that helped these individuals overcome obstacles and thrive in the competitive landscape of the music business.

ARTIST SUCCESS STORY: LIZZO

Background: Lizzo, an American singer, rapper, and flutist, faced numerous challenges before her breakthrough in the music industry. Despite her talent, she struggled to find a mainstream audience for years.

Strategies for Success:

Authenticity and Self-Acceptance:

Lizzo's message of body positivity and self-love resonated with many. By embracing her authentic self, she created a strong connection with her audience, distinguishing herself from other artists.

Utilizing Social Media:

Lizzo effectively used platforms like Instagram and TikTok to highlight her personality, music, and performances. This engagement helped build a dedicated fan base long before her mainstream success.

Collaborative Spirit:

She collaborated with various artists and producers, broadening her musical horizons and enhancing her sound. Collaborations not only expanded her reach but also enriched her creative process.

1. **"Rumors" with Cardi B** – A major collaboration in 2021 that blends hip-hop and pop, featuring both artists' distinctive styles.
2. **"Special" Remix with SZA** – Released in 2023, this remix of Lizzo's hit "Special" features SZA and received praise for its empowering lyrics and harmonious vocals.

Outcome: Lizzo's album *Cuz, I Love You* received critical acclaim, leading to multiple Grammy nominations and a devoted following. Her journey exemplifies the importance of authenticity, social engagement, and collaboration in achieving success.

PRODUCER SUCCESS STORY: PHARRELL WILLIAMS

Background: Pharrell Williams began his career as a producer and songwriter, eventually becoming a global superstar in his own right. He faced challenges breaking into the industry and establishing his brand.

Strategies for Success:

Diverse Skill Set:

Pharrell developed a wide range of skills, including production, songwriting, and fashion design. This versatility allowed him to collaborate across genres and mediums, setting him apart from other producers.

Innovative Collaborations:

He worked with a diverse array of artists, from pop icons like Britney Spears to hip-hop legends like Jay-Z. By blending different musical styles, Pharrell created unique sounds that appealed to various audiences.

Brand Building:

Pharrell successfully built his brand by embracing his individuality and engaging in various ventures, including fashion and philanthropy. His brand became synonymous with creativity and innovation.

Outcome: Pharrell has received multiple Grammy Awards and accolades for his work, and he continues to influence music, fashion, and culture. His story emphasizes the power of diversification, collaboration, and personal branding.

MANAGER SUCCESS STORY: SCOOTER BRAUN

Background: Scooter Braun is a prominent talent manager known for his work with artists like Justin Bieber, Ariana Grande, and many others. He started from humble beginnings, managing a few local artists before making a name for himself in the industry.

Strategies for Success:

Vision and Perseverance:

Braun had a sharp vision of what he wanted to achieve and worked tirelessly to pursue it. He famously discovered Justin Bieber on YouTube and saw potential where others did not.

Building Relationships:

He focused on building strong relationships with artists, fostering a sense of trust and collaboration. Braun's approach emphasizes the importance of understanding artists' needs and aspirations.

Leveraging Technology:

Scooter utilized social media and online platforms to promote his artists, recognizing the changing landscape of music distribution. His forward-thinking approach helped catapult his clients to fame.

Outcome: Scooter Braun became one of the most successful managers in the music industry, significantly impacting the careers of several top artists. His story illustrates the value of vision, relationship-building, and adapting to technological advancements.

4. PRODUCER AND ARTIST COLLABORATION: THE NEPTUNES

Background: The Neptunes, comprised of Pharrell Williams and Chad Hugo, are a legendary production duo known for their innovative sound in the early 2000s. They produced hits for a wide range of artists, shaping the sound of pop and hip-hop.

Strategies for Success:

Distinctive Sound:

The Neptunes developed a unique sound characterized by catchy hooks and innovative beats. They consistently pushed creative boundaries, experimenting with new techniques and styles.

Collaboration and Trust:

They collaborated closely with artists, building trust and allowing for creative freedom. This collaborative spirit led to some of the biggest hits of the era.

Their production credits include Jay-Z's *"I Just Wanna Love U (Give It 2 Me)"* (2000), which blended hip-hop with their signature sound, and Britney Spears' *"I'm a Slave 4 U"* (2001), showcasing their versatility in pop music. They also produced Nelly's summer anthem *"Hot in Herre"* (2002), which became a major hit. The duo's work with Clipse on *"Grindin'"* (2002) highlighted their minimalist style, while their remix of Depeche Mode's *"Dream On"* (2001) demonstrated their ability to cross into electronic music. These collaborations reflect The Neptunes' unique ability to shape various genres, leaving a lasting impact on the music industry.

Branding as a Duo:

The Neptunes effectively branded themselves as a production team, which increased their marketability and appeal to artists seeking a fresh sound.

Outcome: The Neptunes produced numerous chart-topping hits and received multiple Grammy Awards. Their success highlights the power of creativity, collaboration, and a distinctive brand identity in the music industry.

CONCLUSION: LEARNING FROM THE CHAMPIONS

The stories of Lizzo, Pharrell Williams, Scooter Braun, and The Neptunes exemplify the diverse paths to success in the music industry. Each champion faced challenges and utilized unique strategies to overcome them. As aspiring producers, artists, and managers, you can draw inspiration from their journeys, applying their lessons to your path in the music business.

Questions to Challenge the Reader:

1. What qualities do you admire most in the successful individuals featured in this chapter? How can you embody those qualities in your own career?
2. Reflect on the challenge you are currently facing. How can you apply the strategies discussed in these stories to overcome that challenge?
3. Who is some industry figures you admire? Consider reaching out to them for mentorship or insights—what would you ask them if given the opportunity?
4. In what ways can you leverage technology and social media to enhance your brand or the artists you work with?
5. Think about a collaboration you would like to pursue. How can you build relationships that lead to successful partnerships in the industry?

CHAPTER 10:
LEARNING FROM MISTAKES

In any competitive field, the path to success is paved with both triumphs and setbacks. Just as athletes can analyze game footage to learn from both victories and defeats, music industry professionals can gain invaluable insights from their experiences. This chapter explores various case studies that highlight the importance of analyzing both successes and failures, emphasizing continuous improvement and adaptability as key components of a thriving career.

CASE STUDY: THE RISE AND FALL OF A MUSIC LABEL

Background: A once-prominent independent record label rose to fame in the early 2000s, nurturing breakout artists and producing chart-topping hits. However, due to poor management decisions and failure to adapt to changing industry dynamics, the label faced bankruptcy.

Lessons Learned:

Adaptability to Change:

The label struggled to embrace digital distribution and streaming platforms. This oversight led to a significant decline in revenue as fans moved to platforms that the label did not leverage.

Financial Management:

Poor financial planning and overextending investments without secure revenue streams resulted in mounting debts. Effective budgeting and financial forecasting are essential for sustaining a business.

Market Awareness:

The label failed to recognize shifts in audience preferences and trends, highlighting the importance of staying informed about market dynamics—much like a coach analyzing opposing teams to adapt their game plan.

Key Takeaway: Continuous market analysis and adaptability are vital for survival in the evolving landscape of the music industry, akin to how successful teams adapt to their opponents.

CASE STUDY: THE IMPACT OF SOCIAL MEDIA

Background: In the early 2000s, an independent record label emerged as a powerhouse in the music industry, quickly gaining recognition for its innovative approach to artist development and its roster of breakout talents. With several chart-topping hits and an enthusiastic fan base, the label was on a promising trajectory. However, by the mid-2010s, the label faced financial instability and eventually declared bankruptcy.

The fall of the label can be traced back to a series of poor management decisions, a failure to adapt to the rapidly changing music landscape, and financial missteps that led to overwhelming debt. Despite early success, the label's inability to pivot with new industry trends, such as the rise of digital streaming, spelled its eventual collapse.

Lessons Learned:

Adaptability to Change:

The label's refusal to embrace digital distribution and streaming platforms was one of its fatal flaws. While competitors were capitalizing on the shift to platforms like Spotify and Apple Music, this label remained focused on traditional album sales and radio airplay. As a result, it saw a significant drop in revenue as fans turned to platforms the label had neglected.

The key lesson here is the importance of embracing change and staying ahead of the technological curve.

Financial Management:

The label made several reckless financial decisions, including overextending investments in artist contracts without ensuring consistent revenue streams. It also failed to create a sustainable financial model that could withstand market fluctuations. Over time, this led to mounting debts, which were not effectively managed, contributing to the label's bankruptcy. The lesson here is that solid financial planning and risk assessment are crucial to any business's longevity.

Market Awareness:

The label's failure to stay in tune with evolving audience tastes and trends was another critical misstep. It continued to focus on the same genre of music and style, even as consumer preferences shifted toward more digital friendly and genre-blending sounds. The label's failure to recognize these shifts—much like a coach failing to adjust their strategy based on their opponent's play—led to a steady decline in relevance and fan engagement.

Key Takeaway: This case emphasizes the need for constant market analysis, adaptability, and strategic financial management. Like any successful sports team, staying informed, continuously evolving, and adapting to the environment is crucial for long-term success.

CASE STUDY: THE FALL OF A SUPERSTAR

Background: A chart-topping pop star faced public backlash and a significant dip in their career due to controversies surrounding their behavior. This period of struggle resulted in a temporary hiatus from music.

Lessons Learned:

Brand Management:

Just as athletes must carefully manage their public image to avoid negative press, the star's failure to align their public persona with their artistic identity led to a disconnect with fans.

Mental Health Awareness:

Acknowledging the toll of industry pressures on their mental health mirrors how athletes prioritize mental well-being and seek support from coaches and trainers.

Rebuilding Reputation:

Upon returning to the public eye, **Justin Bieber** focused on rebuilding his reputation through transparency, using his platform to advocate for mental health awareness. He shared personal stories about his struggles with fame, mental health, and how he overcame them, connecting with fans who were facing similar challenges. This approach is like how athletes use personal setbacks or challenges to spark social change or inspire their fans. By openly discussing his journey, Bieber was able to foster deeper emotional connections with his fanbase and transform a difficult period into an opportunity for growth.

Key Takeaway:

Navigating personal and professional pressures requires self-awareness, support, and proactive management of one's brand, just like how athletes rely on coaches and teammates for guidance during tough times. By openly addressing past struggles and using his platform for advocacy, Justin Bieber demonstrated the power of vulnerability and growth in rebuilding public trust.

CASE STUDY: COLLABORATING FOR GROWTH

Background: A seasoned producer faced stagnation in their career, with fewer opportunities to collaborate with new artists. Realizing the need for change, they began collaborating with up-and-coming producers and artists.

Lessons Learned:

Embracing New Talent:

Collaborating with emerging talent revitalized the producer's sound and opened new avenues for creativity.

Networking and Relationships:

This experience underscored the value of building relationships, much like how athletes' network within their sport to gain visibility and opportunities.

Continuous Learning:

The producer recognized that continuous learning and adaptation are vital for remaining relevant, just as athletes continuously refine their skills through training and competition.

Key Takeaway: Collaboration and openness to innovative ideas can lead to growth and innovation, helping established professionals stay relevant, like how seasoned athletes learn from younger players.

CONCLUSION: THE PATH TO CONTINUOUS IMPROVEMENT

Learning from mistakes is a fundamental aspect of growth in any industry, particularly in the major music business. By analyzing both successes and failures, just as athletes do through game footage, industry professionals can develop a nuanced understanding of what works and what does not. Embracing a mindset of continuous improvement not only fosters resilience but also enhances creativity and adaptability.

Questions to Challenge the Reader:

1. Reflect on a recent setback in your career. What specific lessons can you extract from this experience, like how an athlete would review game performance?
2. How can you create a culture of feedback within your team or collaborations? What steps will you take to solicit and utilize constructive criticism, akin to a coach's feedback during practice?
3. Consider a failure by a well-known artist or producer. What could they have done differently, and how can you apply those lessons to your own career?
4. How do you manage your public image and brand? Are there areas where you could improve or align more closely with your artistic identity, like how athletes develop their public personas?
5. In what ways can you embrace collaboration to enhance your growth and creativity in the music industry, much like a team working together to achieve a common goal?

CHAPTER 11:
BUILDING A LEGACY

As we wrap up this playbook, it is essential to recognize that building a legacy in the major music industry requires foresight, resilience, and an unwavering commitment to growth. Just as athletes strive to leave their mark through records, championships, and community involvement, major music producers can shape the future of music and influence generations of artists.

The Power of Vision

An unobstructed vision is the foundation of a successful career. This vision should encompass not only the music you want to create but also the impact you wish to have on the industry. Take inspiration from the greats in both music and sports who have not only mastered their craft but have also utilized their platforms to affect positive change. This might mean advocating for up-and-coming talent, pushing for fair industry practices, or simply sharing knowledge through mentorship.

RESILIENCE IN THE FACE OF CHALLENGES

The journey in the major music industry is fraught with challenges—be it evolving technology, shifting market trends, or personal setbacks. Embracing resilience is crucial; it is about learning from failures and using them as steppingstones. Every top major producer has faced moments of doubt and adversity, but those who persist are the ones who carve out their legacies.

COMMITMENT TO CONTINUOUS LEARNING

Just as athletes continuously hone their skills through training and analysis, so too must producers commit to lifelong learning. Staying informed about industry changes, recent technologies, and evolving musical trends can set you apart. Attend workshops, network with peers, and seek feedback to refine your craft.

Personal Experience

Reflecting on my own journey, I recall the early days when every setback felt monumental. Yet, each experience taught me invaluable lessons about the importance of resilience and adaptability. By embracing a growth mindset and seeking to learn from every project, I was able to build lasting relationships and a reputation that opened doors to new opportunities.

Call to Action

As you move forward in your career, remember that you have the power to shape not only your future but the future of the music industry as well. Strive for excellence, advocate for fairness, and never underestimate the influence you can have on those around you. The path may be challenging, but with passion and determination, you can leave a legacy that resonates for years to come.

In closing, your journey as a music producer is just beginning. Embrace it with enthusiasm, integrity, and a willingness to collaborate. The world is waiting for your unique voice and vision—let it be heard.

Questions to Challenge the Reader:

1. What is your long-term vision as a music producer? How can you align your current projects with this vision to build a legacy?
2. In what ways can you commit to ongoing learning and professional development? Are there specific skills or knowledge areas you wish to explore further?
3. Reflect on a producer or artist whose legacy you admire. What elements of their journey resonate with you, and how can you incorporate those lessons into your own career?
4. How can you engage with and support emerging talent in your community? What steps will you take to become a mentor or advocate for new artists?
5. Consider the values that are important to you in your career. How can you ensure that your actions and decisions reflect these values, contributing to a legacy of integrity and respect in the industry?

Final Thoughts Building a legacy in the major music industry is a multifaceted endeavor that requires vision, continuous learning, and a commitment to nurturing others. By embracing these principles, producers can leave an indelible mark on the industry, ensuring that their contributions resonate far beyond their own careers.

Much like sports figures who inspire future generations, major music producers have the unique opportunity to shape the narrative of music, one project at a time. The path may be challenging, but the rewards—both personal and communal—are immeasurable.

CHAPTER 12:
OBSTACLES TO PAYMENT:
THE MUSIC PRODUCER'S ENEMY

In the music industry, producers often find themselves facing two powerful and often overlooked obstacles on their path to financial success: the artist's lawyer and the label's A&R Administration and vendor departments. While these entities might seem like routine parts of the process, they represent major obstacles that, when mismanaged, can delay payments, create roadblocks for success, and leave the producer in a position where they are unable to get paid for their hard work.

THE ARTIST'S LAWYER: GATEKEEPER OF DELAYS

The artist's lawyer may seem like an ally, working in the best interest of the artist. However, what many producers fail to realize is that the artist's lawyer often holds the keys to a deal moving forward—deliberately or otherwise. Unlike the producer, who depends on timely payments to continue their work, with A-list artist lawyer often has secure payment from the label upfront. The B-list and C-list artist lawyers may negotiate a legal fund from which to get paid for clearing an artist's project. It's typically not paid out until the lawyer delivers all the fully executed agreements.

This creates an imbalance particularly for the A-list artist lawyer, who has the luxury of delaying the process, making excuses, and slowing down the momentum of a deal because they've already been paid!

Here's where things get tricky: the term "industry standard" is often used to justify these delays. What does this really mean? The industry standard in many cases is to have the producer sign the agreement first—before the artist even gets involved. Once the producer signs, the agreement is technically considered "partially executed," and the terms agreed-to by the producer. However, this leaves the producer in a vulnerable position, because the record gets released based upon the artist's reliance on the producer's "good faith" approval of the terms and the producer having already signed the agreement with little leverage ensuring that the deal moves forward to closure. The producer will often have to chase down the artist's signature—a task that can take weeks, months and sometimes years!

The artist's lawyer may have good reasons to stall a deal, but none of these are particularly relevant to the producer. They may offer reasons or scenarios like the following:

1. The artist is independent and does not have the cash to pay an advance, so the artist asks the attorney to stall execution
2. The artist is signed to a major label, and they have a roll out plan and the label's delivery requirements include a release date.
3. The artist has a meager budget and wants to make sure they invest in the right song, so they will delay signing a producer agreement because they want to finish a different song and "compare" them.
4. The artist is signed to a major. They like the song, but the label's A&R does not. They have creative differences, and the artist then must stall, completing the producer's agreement until a resolution is met.
5. The artist being on tour and it's difficult to make them sit down to handle business. I've experienced this firsthand. Their adrenaline is high, they are in their creative zones, and egos can go off the charts. Signing a producer agreement may be the last thing on their minds.

Regardless of the excuse, and even if the artist's attorney has NO personal incentive to delay, these delays can go on indefinitely, keeping the producer from receiving their well-earned royalties. The producer cannot collect mechanical or master royalties from the label until the agreement is fully executed and registered with the label. The producer cannot even collect digital performance royalties from Sound Exchange without a signed letter of direction!

So, without a fully executed agreement, the music is locked out from the payment process, preventing the artist and the producer from receiving their fair share of the proceeds. The artist and the label could hold your music hostage!

The Label's A&R Administration and Vendor Department: Another Formidable Obstacle

What many producers do not realize is that the label's payout and registration departments also stand in the way of timely payment. While the producer may have already signed their portion of the agreement, the label will not process any advances or royalties if due until a fully executed agreement—signed by all parties—is submitted. Even after the agreement is fully executed, the label often drags its feet, claiming that they are "understaffed" or too busy to process the advance or royalty payments. The result is that payments are delayed, leaving the producer—and sometimes the artist—waiting for months without receiving what they are owed.

The label's vendor department is notorious for being slow and inefficient. After receiving a partially executed agreement, the producer can expect to be met with a barrage of generic, unhelpful responses like, "Your request has been received. Someone will get back to you shortly." These promises of a response often result in nothing. In many cases, producers spend weeks, if not months, trying to get a clear answer on when their royalties will be processed.

This level of delay is unacceptable, but it is an unfortunate reality for the industry. The label has all the time in the world to delay payments, while the producer is left chasing every step of the process.

THE IMPACT OF THESE DELAYS

So, what does this mean for the producer? To recap, until the agreement is fully executed and processed, the producer cannot get paid. This includes both the primary royalties and any other potential income streams, such as Sound Exchange royalties. A fully executed "Letter of Direction" (LOD) is necessary for the producer to receive their share of digital royalties from services like Spotify, Apple Music, and others. Without the signed LOD, which directs Sound Exchange to pay the producer, the producer is left empty-handed.

What is particularly frustrating is the artist's lawyer is at the negotiating table securing the best possible deal for the artist, while the producer is often left with nothing—waiting and watching as the delay continues.

Personal Experience

I remember a time when I represented a promising young producer who had collaborated with a major artist on a track that quickly became a chart topping hit. We had agreed on the terms, but the artist's lawyer kept stalling on getting the artist's signature. Excuses piled up: "They're on tour," "They are not available," "The artist is unavailable to sign right now." Weeks turned into months, and the track was already out in the world, generating revenue, but my producer was left unpaid.

Despite multiple follow-ups, the artist's lawyer continued to use every excuse in the book to avoid getting the signature we needed. At this point, we had no choice but to push back and challenge the so-called "industry standard" that the producer's signature came first. We insisted that the artist sign first, and that became the game-changer. Only after the artist's signature was obtained did the label begin processing royalties for everyone involved. It took months, but we finally got the payment my producer deserved. The experience was a harsh lesson in the reality of the business. It reinforced the importance of being proactive, demanding accountability, and challenging the standard practices that routinely disadvantage producers.

THE "INDUSTRY STANDARD" IS NOT ALWAYS YOUR FRIEND

You would think that if the artist signed first and then the producer, the deal would be fully executed, and the labels could register it in their system for immediate royalty payment. However, the "industry standard" works in the opposite direction, and delays are used to the advantage of the artist and their team. The truth is that the artist's lawyer has no urgency to push the deal through quickly. The standard practice is to drag out the process as long as possible, using excuses like understaffed departments or the label's unresponsive royalty teams.

A producer's job, therefore, is to stay vigilant. Do not let days, weeks, or months go by without following up. You must stay on top of the process, and do not allow the artist's lawyer or the label to control the narrative. In the world of major music, the artist's lawyer works in tandem with the label, and they both know the value of time and delays. For a producer trying to build a career, those delays are costly.

Key Takeaways:

- Understand the power of the artist's lawyer in controlling the pace of the deal.

- Insist on the artist signing first, and make sure all documents are fully executed before any work proceeds.

- Never accept vague excuses—chase down the signatures, track down the paperwork, and follow up relentlessly.

- Be proactive about getting your royalties, including pushing for the signature on the Letter of Direction (LOD) to ensure you are paid directly by Sound Exchange.

- The "industry standard" may often be used as a way to delay payments and keep producers from getting what they're owed. It is up to you to challenge these norms and demand what is rightfully yours.

Remember: As a music producer, you are not just a musician, you are also a business professional. Protect your work and your compensation. The more prepared you are for these hurdles, the more successfully you will navigate the complexities of the major music industry. Be ready to push back when necessary and do not settle for "industry standard" delays that harm your career.

Questions to Challenge the Reader:

1. **Identifying Roadblocks**

   Reflect on a situation where a lawyer or label department delayed your payment or progress. What specific steps could you have taken to mitigate the issue?

2. **Challenging "Industry Standards"**

   Have you encountered an "industry standard" practice that worked against your interests? How could you challenge these practices to better protect your rights?

3. **Ensuring Agreement Clarity**

   How often do you review contract terms before signing, and what areas do you tend to overlook? How can you strengthen your process to ensure agreements are in your favor?

4. **Avoiding Bottlenecks with Lawyers and Labels**

   What strategies can you implement to minimize delays from lawyers or label departments? Have you tried alternative methods to speed up communication or approvals?

5. **Understanding Fully Executed Agreements**

   Are you familiar with the steps needed to ensure a fully executed agreement? What checkpoints can you add to verify that all necessary parties sign agreements?

6. **Advocating for Your Rights**

   How comfortable are you with insisting on terms that protect your rights, such as who should sign first? What support systems or resources could help you feel more confident?

7. **Communicating Effectively with Lawyers**

   When dealing with lawyers who delay responses, how can you communicate in a way that maintains professionalism but asserts urgency? Are there specific phrases or tactics you find effective?

8. **Staying Persistent in Follow-Ups**

    Describe a follow-up strategy that could prevent delays in agreement finalization. How can you consistently check in without feeling like you are pestering?

9. **Protecting Against Unauthorized Releases**

    What steps can you take to avoid unauthorized releases of your work? Do you know the protocols for issuing takedown notice if necessary?

10. **Reflecting on Personal Experiences**

    Have you ever encountered situations like those described in this chapter? How did they shape your approach to contracts, lawyers, and label departments?

CHAPTER 13: TIME WASTERS

RECOGNIZING AND AVOIDING THE PITFALLS IN MAJOR MUSIC BUSINESS

In the major music industry, as in life, time is one of your most valuable assets. As a major music producer, your focus should be on creating music, building relationships, and pushing your career forward. Unfortunately, there are people in the industry who thrive on distractions and delays, leading to nothing more than wasting time. These time-wasters exist in every corner of the business—whether it is in the form of artists, managers, or even other producers—and they can be as detrimental to your success as an unmotivated player on an NBA team.

In the NBA, teams invest millions of dollars in players, but if a player is not focused, dedicated, or willing to put in the work, they become a liability to the team. Similarly, in the major music industry, you will encounter individuals who promise the world but fail to deliver results. Just as a team coach or general manager would cut ties with an underperforming player, it is critical for you as a producer to identify these time wasters early and make swift decisions to protect your time and career.

IDENTIFYING TIME WASTERS: THE NBA COMPARISON

Imagine a scenario where an NBA team invests in a young player with tons of potential, but the player constantly shows up late to practice, does not take advice from the coaching staff, and fails to improve over time. That player would quickly be labeled a "time-waster," and no matter how much potential they had, they would be sidelined or traded. In the world of music production, this scenario plays out regularly.

For instance, you might get approached by an artist or manager who seems eager to collaborate with you. They have grandiose ideas and a grand vision for collaboration. But after multiple meetings and countless hours spent discussing plans, you realize that they are simply not putting in the work to back up their words. They miss deadlines, fail to communicate effectively, or never deliver on promises. This is the music industry's version of a "bench player" who fails to contribute.

In both professional sports and the music industry, results are what matter. No matter how talented a player or artist may be, if they do not deliver, they will be left behind. The key difference between a star player and a time waster is their commitment to consistent improvement and tangible results.

THE MUSIC PRODUCER'S TIME WASTERS

1.The Promiser Who Never Delivers:

In the music industry, you will inevitably encounter individuals who have all the right connections, grand vision, and promises of success. These "dreamers" make you believe that a deal or collaboration is just around the corner—one signature away from a breakthrough. They exaggerate potential projects with enthusiasm, describing a future where you are working with top-tier artists, major labels, and influential industry figures. The problem? When it is time to act and execute the plans they have promised, they fall short. These are the Promisers: people who speak in bold terms but fail to back up their words with tangible results.

Their inability to follow through can drain your time, energy, and resources, all while leaving you in a constant state of uncertainty. Every promise they make comes with an invisible expiration date, and once that time lapses without progress, you are left wondering if you were ever truly on the right path.

Example:

You meet an artist who claims they have a major-label backing and are ready to launch a collaboration with you that will put you on the map. They talk about the connections they have, the executive meetings they have had, and how their deal with the label is about to close.

They promise a fast track to success, urging you to invest time, energy, and even some upfront costs into the project. The excitement builds, and you sign on the dotted line, convinced that this is the opportunity for which you have been waiting.

But weeks pass, then months, and still, nothing happens. You reach out for updates, but the artist is either too busy or their responses are vague, always promising that the deal is "almost finalized." You notice that the promised label backing never materializes. When you dig deeper, you find out that the artist's deal was not as close to closing as they led you to believe. In fact, they do not have the connections they claimed, and their "major backing" may be nothing more than smoke and mirrors.

The project stalls because they were not truly ready to follow through. Meanwhile, you have invested valuable time and energy in an empty promise, making no real progress in your career. The worst part is that it was not just time wasted, it was the emotional tool of believing in something that was never a sure thing.

You find yourself reflecting on how easily you were convinced by someone who talked a good game but failed to deliver on any of the promises.

The Emotional Toll:

The "Promiser Who Never Delivers" can have a serious impact on your motivation and mental state. You start second-guessing your instincts and wondering if you are too trusting. These individuals can cause self-doubt, as you question whether you are chasing the wrong opportunities or if you are just not cut out for the industry. The more you invest in their promises, the harder it becomes to walk away, because you are already emotionally and professionally invested in the idea of success they painted for you.

How to Protect Yourself:

- **Verify Their Claims.** Do not just take someone's word for it. Always verify their connections, claims, and leverage. In the music business, who you know matters, but it is essential to ensure that those "connections" are real and tangible.
- **Get Everything in Writing.** If someone is serious about a project, they will be willing to put it in writing. A signed contract is your best protection against unfulfilled promises.
- **Follow Up Regularly.** Do not let things slide. If you have not heard from them in a while, send regular check-ins. A professional who is serious about the project will stay in communication with you and keep things moving forward.
- **Do not Be Afraid to Walk Away.** If the promises keep being delayed and there is no progress, it is time to walk away. There are always other opportunities, and wasting time on empty promises is the quickest way to stall your career.

The Key Takeaway:

The Promiser Who Never Delivers might offer the illusion of an opportunity, but their lack of follow-through can result in significant lost time and energy. While their promises can seem convincing at first, their inability to execute can leave you stuck in an endless cycle of waiting. To protect your career, make sure you are collaborating with individuals who can back up their words with action. In this industry, your time is too valuable to waste on promises that never come true. Trust is earned through action, not words.

2. The Chronic Talker:

These individuals are experts in persuasion, gifted in the art of storytelling and selling grandiose ideas. They know how to captivate you with grand visions of success, charm you with their enthusiasm, and make you believe that they hold the key to unlocking your next big break. Whether it is a publishing deal, a collaboration with a major artist, or a connection to an influential industry figure, they paint a picture of limitless possibilities.

But when it comes time to turn their words into action, the Chronic Talker falls short. Instead of delivering on their promises, they stall, delay decisions, push back timelines, and change their minds constantly, leaving you in a perpetual state of uncertainty and frustration.

What makes this behavior so dangerous is that it is not just about empty promises, it is about the wasted time and emotional energy you invest in them. The Chronic Talker knows how to make you feel like you are on the verge of something great, only to leave you stranded in a never-ending loop of waiting. In the music business, time is one of your most valuable assets. Every moment spent with someone who is all talk, and no action is time you could be spending moving forward with a partner who is invested in your success.

Example:

Think of a manager who promises you a publishing deal after several meetings. They convince you that they have all the right connections, the industry knowledge, and the experience to get the deal done. They talk about a big game, telling you about all the other clients they have helped, the labels they are in contact with, and how quickly they can make things happen for you. They sell you on a future that sounds too good to pass up, and you start to believe that they are the missing link in your career.

But when it comes time to act—when it is time to put things into writing, set up meetings with the label, or push the deal forward, nothing happens.

They delay, reschedule, and provide vague excuses: "Oh, the label is backlogged," "They are waiting for a response from the artist," or "We just need a bit more time to fine-tune the details." Days turn into weeks, and weeks turn into months, and still, you are left with nothing but empty promises. This is no different from a coach who fills his locker room with motivational speeches and promises of championship glory but fails to execute the plays that would win the game.

The Chronic Talker leaves you stuck, unable to progress because they do not follow through on their words. They are happy to tell you what you want to hear, but when it comes to delivering results, they are nowhere to be found. You end up questioning whether they ever intended to help you succeed in the first place, or if they were just looking to use your time to fuel their own ego or business.

The Impact on Your Career:

In the fast-paced and competitive world of the music industry, time is crucial. Every day spent waiting on the Chronic Talker is a day you could have spent forging ahead with a serious, committed partner. Their behavior can cause you to lose out on other opportunities, as you waste time waiting for someone who never fully delivers. As you chase their empty promises, other producers, artists, and industry professionals who act will continue to build their careers, leaving you behind.

Your reputation as a producer is built on your ability to deliver results, not just ideas. If you get caught up in the cycle of waiting on the Chronic "Talker," you risk falling behind and getting lost in the noise of unfulfilled promises.

The Key Takeaway:

The Chronic Talker may offer you the illusion of opportunity, but they often fail to deliver tangible results. You must be vigilant in recognizing when you are dealing with someone who plays a big game but lacks the ability or commitment to follow through. If someone's words are not backed by actions, it is time to move on. The music industry is full of opportunities, but only if you are willing to invest your time and energy in people who are as committed to making things happen as you are.

How to Protect Yourself:

- **Get everything in writing.** If someone is serious about collaborating with you, they will be willing to formalize the agreement and make real moves.
- **Be wary of excuses.** If you hear the same reason for delays repeatedly, it is time to assess whether this person is really invested in helping you move forward.
- **Hold them accountable.** Set deadlines and ask for tangible results. If they keep pushing back the timeline without providing substantial reasons, it is a red flag.
- **Do not be afraid to walk away.** There are plenty of professionals who are eager to collaborate with you and are willing to take real steps to help your career grow. Do not waste time on someone who is not serious.

In the music business, your career is too important to be left in the hands of the Chronic "Talker." Recognize the difference between someone who can help you grow and someone who is simply filling the air with empty words. Be strategic with your time and your partnerships and focus on those who will turn their talk into action.

3. The Popular Major Music Producer:

Some popular major music producers may initially reach out with excitement and enthusiasm. However, as time goes on, it becomes evident that these producers may not be fully engaged in entering a professional, high-level collaboration. Instead, they are more interested in low-effort, one-off collaborations, work-for-hire deals, or even fleeting publishing/admin agreements. These producers may not be committed to the long-term, strategic partnership you are hoping for, and this can waste valuable time as you hold out for a breakthrough that may never come. They love the idea of collaborating with rising stars but lack the dedication to make it truly happen on a professional level.

Example:

You are approached by a popular major music producer who wants to use your melody for a high-profile record they are working on with a major label artist. The producer promises a 50/50 split on the collaboration and insists that this track is going to "blow up" and put both of you on the map. Initially, the excitement is palpable. The promise of a big collaboration with an established producer is an excellent opportunity. You both talk about the vision for the track, the potential for it to chart, and the exposure it could bring. But when it comes time to put things in writing, the terms of the deal shift. Suddenly, you are not hearing back as often, and when you do, the producer is distracted with other projects.

After several rounds of back-and-forth, you realize the original promise of a 50/50 split has changed to a smaller percentage, with additional clauses that benefit the producer more than you. Instead of collaborating on the track as partners, they are now treating it as a work-for-hire project, giving you less ownership and influence.

The cold truth? This producer is simply not as committed to the long-term partnership that they initially pitched. They are looking for quick wins rather than cultivating lasting, mutually beneficial professional relationships. They know they hold the power and leverage in the situation—after all, they are the established name in the room, the one with access to the big artists and labels, while you are still climbing the ladder. What they fail to realize is that their inability to follow through on their promises is robbing you of the chance to build something lasting.

The Impact on Your Career:

This kind of situation can be frustrating and disheartening, especially if you are an aspiring producer looking for a breakthrough. It is not just the missed opportunity; it is the mental and emotional toll that these false promises and delays take on you. You may spend weeks or even months waiting for this collaboration to materialize, while your time and energy could have been better spent building more meaningful partnerships with producers, artists, or labels who are genuinely invested in your career.

Furthermore, this behavior can harm your professional reputation. As a music producer, you are only as strong as the deals you make and the relationships you build. If the word gets out that you have been left in the dust by a major producer, it could deter other artists or producers from collaborating with you. In a highly competitive industry, your reputation and your network are crucial to your success. Time spent waiting for a collaboration that never fully materializes is time you will never get back.

The Key Takeaway:

When dealing with major music producers, always protect your time and your value. If someone promises you a partnership but does not follow through with professional paperwork and commitment, recognize the warning signs early. Do not let them waste your time with vague promises that may never materialize. Staying vigilant in getting everything in writing upfront—collaborative agreements should always be formalized before the music is made, not after the fact. If they are not willing to put the work into securing the deal professionally, it is likely they are more interested in taking what they can from the situation without giving you your fair due.

HOW TO PROTECT YOURSELF:

Some artists may reach out with enthusiasm, but it becomes clear that they are not fully prepared to enter into a professional agreement or oversee the planning that comes with making music at a prominent level. These artists may lack a work ethic, organization, or basic understanding of the industry, which means you end up spending more time babysitting than producing. At the end of the day, the major producer who is not fully committed is not the type of partner you want to invest your time and effort in. Focus on building relationships with people who are just as enthusiastic and dedicated to your mutual success as you are. Only then will you begin to see the kind of long-term, fruitful partnerships that drive your career forward.

HOW TO AVOID TIME WASTERS

1. **Set Clear Expectations:**
   Just as an NBA coach would set clear goals and expectations for a player, you should do the same with anyone you collaborate with. Be upfront with timelines, roles, and deliverables so that everyone knows what is expected of them.

2. **Evaluate Commitment:**

   Just as a team scout watches potential players to see how they perform under pressure, take note of how your collaborators react when faced with deadlines, challenges, or changes. Are they proactive and committed to the process, or do they start backing out when things get tough?

3. **Limit Overly Lengthy Meetings:**

   You do not need endless meetings to understand whether a person is serious or not. If someone consistently shows up unprepared or fails to execute their promises, it is time to cut your losses and move on.

4. **Stay Focused on Results:**

   Like a coach who evaluates players based on performance, always keep your eye on the results. If someone is not delivering tangible results, even if they talk a big game, it is time to consider whether they are worth your time.

5. **Trust Your Instincts:**

   Trust your gut when it comes to working with others. If something feels off, or if the person seems more interested in talking than doing, do not be afraid to walk away.

CONCLUSION:

In both professional sports and the major music industry, time is everything. Time wasted on uncommitted people is time you could be investing in your craft, building real relationships, and progressing in your career. The key to success is knowing who is worth your time and who is not. As a music producer, you must have the discipline to cut ties with time wasters early and focus on those who will elevate your career and produce tangible results.

Your career as a producer depends on how you manage your time and resources. So, avoid the distractions, cut the dead weight, and stay focused on what matters. After all, you do not want to be remembered as the producer who spent years chasing empty promises—just like you do not want to be the NBA team that invested in a player who never lived up to their potential.

Questions to Challenge the Reader:

1. **Recognizing Patterns of Time Wasting**

   Think of a time when you felt your efforts were wasted by a collaborator. What specific behaviors or red flags could you now identify to avoid similar situations?

2. **Establishing Boundaries**

   What boundaries can you set in future collaborations to protect your time and resources? How can you communicate these expectations effectively?

3. **Evaluating Value vs. Hype**

   How do you distinguish between someone who genuinely adds value and someone who only brings hype without substance? Are there specific criteria you use?

4. **Defining Productive Collaborations**

   Reflect on a successful collaboration. What qualities and behaviors made it productive? How can you prioritize these in new projects?

5. **Dealing with Chronic Talkers**

   How can you address a collaborator who constantly talks but does not act? What strategies can you use to keep projects moving forward?

6. **Managing the Promiser Who Never Delivers**

   Have you worked with someone who promised massive things but failed to deliver? What did you learn from this experience, and how can you apply it to future relationships?

7. **Prioritizing Your Own Goals**

   Are you investing time in collaborations that align with your long-term goals, or are you getting sidetracked by unproductive partnerships? How can you refocus on what matters?

8. **Recognizing When to Walk Away**

   How comfortable are you with ending a collaboration that does not serve you? What factors do you consider before deciding to move on?

9. **Improving Screening Processes**

   What new steps can you implement to screen potential collaborators or clients before committing your time?

10. **Building an Accountability Framework**

    How can you establish accountability measures in collaborations to ensure all parties follow through on their promises?

CHAPTER 14:
INDUSTRY STANDARDS

WHY THE NEW STANDARD IS ESSENTIAL

In the major music industry, the term "industry standard" is tossed around as if it is the ultimate rulebook that everyone must follow. But for music producers, many of these outdated norms can work against them, creating roadblocks to getting paid, achieving recognition, and maintaining a sustainable career. In this chapter, we will examine why it is essential for modern producers to push back against these old-school norms and instead adopt a new standard way of working that prioritizes clarity, fairness, and efficiency.

WHY THE "INDUSTRY STANDARD" CAN LIMIT PRODUCERS

Traditional industry standards were established at a time when labels held all power. This meant that royalty payments were often delayed, payment structures were unclear, and contracts heavily favored labels over the creators themselves. For today's producers, following these outdated standards can lead to stalled projects, missed payments, and a lot of wasted time and resources.

THE NEW STANDARD: A PRODUCER'S GUIDE TO FAIR PRACTICES

To avoid the pitfalls of the old ways, producers today need to advocate for themselves by embracing what I call the New Standard. This is not just about avoiding vague contract language; it is about creating practices that protect your work, time, and income. Here is how:

1. **Clear Payment Timelines and Terms:**

   When negotiating, avoid ambiguous phrases like "upon label approval" or "as determined by the label." Specify exact payment dates, ideally within a set number of days after release.

   - **Example in Action:**

     On a recent project, I specified that royalties would be due within 45 days of the song's release date, with late penalties included. Not only did this secure my payment sooner, but it also encouraged the label to prioritize my payout.

   - **Direct Involvement in Contract Drafting:**

     Relying on "standard contracts" can result in major gaps for producers. By getting directly involved in the language and terms, producers can ensure their contributions are valued and protected.

   - **Personal Experience:**

     After my experience of that delayed payout, I began personally reviewing every contract with my lawyer. In one deal, I noticed a clause that allowed the label to "reallocate" marketing funds from production to other expenses. By negotiating to remove that clause, I protected my own budget and avoided any nasty surprises.

2. **Transparency in Royalties and Reporting:**

   Industry standards often allow labels to delay or obscure royalty calculations. The New Standard encourages producers to demand access to regular royalty statements and request audits when numbers seem off. Major music producer agreements should have an audit clause. Take advantage of it and ask for one!

3. **Insisting on Full Execution Before Release:**

   A major industry standard involves allowing songs to be released even if the paperwork is not fully completed, often leading to issues with payment. As part of the New Standard, it is wise to demand full execution of agreements before the track goes live.

   - **Personal Experience:**

     I once worked on a project where the artist's lawyer delayed returning the fully executed contract, even though the track was already live and streaming. Each week that passed meant lost royalties, and the lawyer used vague excuses about the artist being on tour. To avoid this in the future, I've made it a practice to insist on fully executed agreements before allowing any music to be released.

OVERCOMING PUSHBACK ON THE NEW STANDARD

Shifting to new practices does not always come easily, especially when working with major labels and their legal teams. Producers who choose to challenge outdated norms may face pushbacks, but it is important to remember that this resistance is often a way to maintain control. A few strategies can help smooth these conversations:

Build a Team with Backbone:

Your manager and lawyer need to be equally committed to upholding fair standards, and they should be prepared to hold the line during negotiations.

Communicate Firm Expectations:

Remember, the artist is licensing YOUR music! IF they want to use your music, they should have no problem signing first. Clearly outline your expectations upfront, so all parties understand that you are serious about the New Standard.

Questions to Challenge the Reader:

1. **Identifying Outdated Standards**

   Reflect on some of the "industry standards" you have encountered in your career. What specific practices seemed outdated or unhelpful?

2. **Understanding the New Standard**

   What does the "new standard" look like for you as a music producer? How does it better reflect the current industry landscape compared to traditional methods?

3. **Evaluating Your Boundaries**

   Have you ever felt pressured to conform to an outdated standard? How did you overlook it, and would you approach it differently now with a new-standard mindset?

4. **Recognizing When to Adapt**

   What are some key indicators that suggest an industry standard is becoming obsolete? How can you stay flexible and adapt to these changes proactively?

5. **Balancing Tradition with Innovation**

   Are there any traditional practices you feel still hold value in today's industry? How can you incorporate beneficial elements while rejecting those that no longer serve your goals?

6. **Building Confidence to Challenge Norms**

   How comfortable do you feel challenging outdated standards? If this is an area for growth, what steps can you take to become more confident?

7. **Learning from Others' Experiences**

   Who are some peers, mentors, or role models who have successfully shifted away from outdated practices? How can their actions inspire or guide your approach?

8. **Creating a Sustainable Career Path**

   How can adhering to a "new standard" contribute to building a sustainable and fulfilling career? What changes could help you reach this goal?

9. **Strengthening Negotiation Skills**

   What specific skills could help you advocate new, fairer standards in your contracts and collaborations? How can you start building these skills now?

10. **Influencing Industry-Wide Change**

    How can your commitment to a "new standard" impact the music industry as a whole? What steps can you take to be a positive force in helping others adopt these improved practices?

CHAPTER 15:
GLOSSARY OF INDUSTRY TERMS

Here is a list of twenty essential industry terms that major music producers should know, along with their definitions:

1. **A&R (Artists and Repertoire)**: The division of a record label responsible for scouting talent and overseeing the artistic development of artists.
2. **Advance**: An upfront payment made to an artist or producer against future earnings, such as royalties.
3. **Back End**: Refers to the income that is earned after a project is completed, usually through royalties, licensing, and other forms of residuals.
4. **BMI (Broadcast Music, Inc.)**: One of the major Performing Rights Organizations (PROs) in the U.S. that collects licensing fees on behalf of songwriters and publishers.
5. **BPM (Beats Per Minute)**: A measurement of tempo in music, indicating how many beats occur in one minute. This is important for matching the energy of songs in a mix or a set.
6. **Co-Publishing Agreement**: A deal where a songwriter shares ownership of their publishing rights with a publisher, usually in exchange for an advance and a share of royalties.
7. **Cross-Collateralization**: A financial arrangement in which the income from one project is used to recoup expenses from another project.
8. **Demos**: Short recordings created to highlight an artist's or songwriter's work, often used to pitch songs or ideas to producers and labels. **Master Recording**: The original recording of a song or piece of music from which copies are made.

9. **Mechanical Royalties**: Royalties paid to songwriters and publishers for the reproduction of their music on physical formats (like CDs) or digital formats (like downloads).
10. **MDRC (Minimum Delivery and Release Commitment)**: A contractual obligation that specifies the minimum number of songs a producer must deliver to a label within a certain period.
11. **Points**: A term used to describe a percentage of royalties (e.g., "4 points" means 4% of the revenue generated from sales, streams, etc.).
12. **Recoupment**: The process by which a record label or publisher recovers advances paid to artists or producers from their future earnings before they receive additional payments.
13. **PRO (Performing Rights Organization)**: An organization that manages the rights of songwriters and composers, ensuring they are compensated for the public performance of their music.
14. **Royalty Split**: The division of royalties between the parties involved in the creation of a song, often negotiated in advance.
15. **Sync Licensing**: The process of licensing music for use in visual media, such as films, TV shows, commercials, and video games.
16. **Sampling**: The act of taking a portion of a sound recording and reusing it in a different song or piece of music.
17. **Track Sheet**: A document that details the arrangement, instrumentation, and specific details about each track in a session.
18. **Umbrella Agreement**: A comprehensive contract that outlines the general terms and conditions for a working relationship, covering multiple projects.
19. **Work-for-Hire**: A legal term indicating that a creator (like a producer or songwriter) is compensated for their work without retaining rights to the resulting work.

When negotiating contracts and deals in the music industry, it is crucial to be well-versed in terminology that can help you challenge your lawyer or ensure that you are receiving fair treatment. Here are some terms that you might consider using in discussions with your lawyer regarding your deal:

1. **Recoupment**: Question how and when the advance will be recouped. For example, "What specific conditions need to be met for recoupment, and how does that impact my potential earnings?"

2. **Equitable Share**: Use this to ensure that your share of royalties is fair. "What does an equitable share look like for my contributions under this agreement?"

3. **Ownership Rights**: Challenge your lawyer to clarify the ownership stakes involved. "Can you confirm what percentage of ownership I will retain in this agreement?"

4. **Term Length**: Ask about the duration of the contract. "Is the term length reasonable for my current and future projects?"

5. **Exclusivity Clause:** Question any exclusivity terms that may limit your opportunities. "What are the implications of this exclusive clause on my ability to collaborate with other artists?"

6. **Termination Rights:** Ensure you understand your exit options. "What are the termination rights in this contract, and under what conditions can I exit without penalties?"

7. **Human Error:** Reference to ensure your interests are safeguarded against mistakes. "What measures are in place to prevent human error from affecting my royalties or rights?"

8. **Market Value:** Challenge your lawyer to provide context on your worth. "How does this offer compare to current market values for producers of my stature?"

9. **Points and Percentages:** Clarify the percentage to which you are entitled. "How many points am I receiving, and what does that translate into in real dollars?"

10. **Back End Earnings:** Ensure clarity on your future earnings. "Can you explain how back-end earnings are calculated, and how can we protect my interests in future revenue?"

11. **Scope of Work:** Discuss what is included in your role. "Can we clarify the scope of work defined in this contract? Are there any additional expectations?"

12. **Publishing Rights:** Confirm your rights to any publishing income. "What are my publishing rights under this agreement, and how will they be managed?"

13. **Performance Metrics:** Challenge how success is defined. "What metrics will be used to determine success, and how does that impact my compensation?"

14. **Creative Control:** Clarify your input on the project. "What level of creative control do I maintain, and can that be documented in this agreement?"

15. **Collateralization":** Use this term to understand financial arrangements. "Can we discuss how cross-collateralization affects my potential earnings from this deal?"

16. **Liability:** Make sure you understand your risks. "What liability am I assuming in this agreement, and how can we mitigate it?"

17. **Future Commitments:** Challenge any obligations that may affect you later. "What future commitments am I agreeing to in this contract, and are they reasonable?"

18. **"Legal Remedies:** Discuss what actions can be taken in case of a dispute. "What legal remedies are available to me if the terms of this contract are breached?"

19. **Force Majeure:** Understand the implications of unforeseen events. "How does this force majeure clause protect me in case of unforeseen circumstances affecting production?"

20. **Negotiation Flexibility:** Ensure your ability to renegotiate in the future. "Is there room for renegotiation in this contract if circumstances change?"

CHAPTER 16:
SPLIT SHEET TEMPLATE

Here is a blank split sheet template that you can use to outline the contributions and splits for a song among collaborators: By signing, each party agrees to the contribution percentages outlined below.

Also included are some additional elements, so your split sheet can serve as a comprehensive and effective tool for collaboration among music producers, songwriters, and other contributors, minimizing misunderstandings and protecting everyone's interests.

SPLIT SHEET

Song Title: _____

Date: _____

Contributors:

Name	Role (Artist, Producer, Writer)	Contribution Description	Percentage Split (%)
____	_____	_____	_____
____	_____	_____	_____
____	_____	_____	_____
____	_____	_____	_____
____	_____	_____	_____

Total Percentage: 100%

Here are some additional elements and sections you might consider including in your split sheet to make it more comprehensive:

1. **Contact Information**: Add a section for each contributor's contact information, including email addresses and phone numbers. This can be helpful for communication purposes.

2. **Publishing Information**: Include a section for the publishing company or PRO (Performing Rights Organization) associated with each contributor. This ensures clarity regarding how royalties will be managed.

3. **Recording Information**: Add details about where the song was recorded (studio name, location) and any relevant recording dates.

4. **ISRC Code**: Include space for the International Standard Recording Code (ISRC), which helps in tracking the song across various platforms.

5. **Distribution Details**: Consider adding a section to indicate how the song will be distributed, whether through a label, self-release, or another method.

6. **Additional Notes**: A dedicated area for any specific agreements, conditions, or unusual circumstances related to the song or the split.

7. **Termination Clause**: A brief note on what happens if any party wishes to terminate their agreement regarding the splits.

8. **Amendment Process**: A section explaining how any changes to the split should be documented and agreed upon by all parties.

9. **Confirmation of Rights**: A statement confirming that all parties have the right to contribute to the song and that the contributions are original.

10. **Witness Signature**: Space for a witness to sign, adding an additional layer of formality to the agreement.

11. **Percentage Breakdown**: Clearly outline the percentage split for each contributor, with a total at the bottom to confirm that it sums to 100%.

12. **Song Title and Description**: Include the title of the song and a brief description or theme of the song, which can provide contexts for all parties involved.

13. **Session Information**: A section for information about the writing and recording sessions, including dates and locations.

14. **Contributors' Roles**: A detailed breakdown of each contributor's role (e.g., songwriter, producer, vocalist) to clarify responsibilities.

15. **Recoupment Terms**: If applicable, mention how and when the recoupment of any advances or costs will be overseen.

16. **Royalty Payment Schedule**: Include a note on how often royalties will be paid out and under what circumstances.

17. **Dispute Resolution**: A clause outlining how disputes will be resolved (mediation, arbitration, etc.) can help prevent misunderstandings later.

18. **Governing Law**: Specify which jurisdiction's laws govern the agreement in case of any legal issues.

19. **Signature and Date**: Ensure there's space for all parties to sign and date the document, making it official.

20. **Digital Rights Management**: If relevant, include information about how digital rights will be managed and protected.

CHAPTER 17: EMAIL TEMPLATE

EMAIL EXAMPLE TO SEND TO LAWYER

The tone of your email is crucial in establishing and maintaining professional relationships, particularly in the major music industry where clear communication is vital. A well-crafted email tone can convey respect, urgency, or collaboration, depending on the context of your message. For instance, when addressing sensitive matters, such as delays or disagreements, a diplomatic and courteous tone is essential to foster constructive dialogue and avoid unnecessary conflict.

Conversely, when time is of the essence or when addressing serious issues, a more assertive tone may be appropriate to convey the urgency of the situation. Understanding when to adopt a formal tone versus a more casual one can help you navigate different scenarios effectively, whether you are communicating with lawyers, artists, or industry executives. By carefully considering your tone, you not only enhance your professional image but also ensure your message is received in the spirit it was intended, paving the way for positive outcomes and successful collaborations.

Subject: Urgent: Clarification Needed on Contract Delay

Dear [Lawyer's Name],

I hope this message finds you well. I am writing to express my concerns regarding the recent delays in finalizing the terms we discussed. It is extremely baffling to me that we have not yet received a resolution, especially considering that the terms were agreed upon during our last conversation.

As we both know, time is of the essence in the music industry, and any further delays could jeopardize potential opportunities. I would appreciate it if you could provide an update on the status of our agreement and clarify any outstanding issues that might be causing this hold-up.

If there are specific points that require further discussion or negotiation, please let me know. I am eager to move forward and finalize this deal as soon as possible.

Thank you for your attention to this matter. I look forward to your prompt response.

Best regards,

Your Name

CHAPTER 18: FINAL CHALLENGE:

BRINGING IT ALL TOGETHER

As we reach the end of this playbook, take a moment to recognize the power and potential within your hands. The major music industry, like professional sports, is not a game for the faint of heart. It is filled with challenges, from "industry standards" that can work against you to timewasters who drain your energy. But you have chosen to be here, to elevate yourself to the level where your skills, commitment, and resilience can shine. Now, let us look at how to put all of this into practice.

A Personal Reflection: I remember a time when I, too, faced uncertainty. A pivotal moment came when I was in a deal where everyone told me to "follow the standard," to just wait. But waiting was not going to protect my rights or give me the earnings I deserved. I took a step back, challenged the "standard," and pushed for what I knew was fair. That one move redefined my career, proving that the industry standard does not dictate your success—you do. Let this book serve as a reminder that stepping away from norms can be the start of a groundbreaking path.

Your Final Challenge: Bring each lesson to life on your own journey. Here is a takeaway from throughout these crucial chapters you have explored:

1. **Establishing Your Role:**

    Clearly define your role and value to avoid being undervalued or underpaid. Set boundaries, advocate for yourself, and hold others accountable.

2. **Protecting Your Rights:**

   Never settle for "standard" if it risks your intellectual property. Understand every term and know your options if a label, artist, or manager does not honor the deal.

3. **Handling Timewasters:**

   Trust your instincts. If someone repeatedly delays, take control. Sometimes, walking away frees up the time and energy you need for real opportunities.

4. **Breaking the Mold:**

   The New Standard you create for yourself may be the difference between a career that thrives and one that stalls. Push for modern practices, transparency, and fair pay.

In the End: This playbook is your launchpad. Let each chapter inform not just what you do but how you do it. Embrace the challenges, protect your rights, and continually evolve. Remember, real relationships plus real results bring success. So go out there and write your legacy—not just as a producer but as a leader in the music industry.

First, I want to thank God for guiding me throughout this journey. Your strength and grace have been my constant source of inspiration.

I'm grateful to my incredible team: Go Grizzly, Smash David, Pooh Beatz, London Jae, TurnMeUpJosh, Yak Beats, and Legal team. Especially Alicia Ferriabough Taylor who gets things done on the legal side. Thank you, Lisa Davis, Brian Johnston, Mike Caren. Thank you to my team's unwavering support, hard work, and dedication have been invaluable in bringing this project to life. I couldn't have done this without each of you.

www.ingramcontent.com/pod-product-compliance
Lightning Source LLC
Chambersburg PA
CBHW061650120626
46550CB00003B/896